Good Morning, GOD!

180 DEVOTIONAL PRAYERS FOR WOMEN

CAREY SCOTT

BARBOUR
PUBLISHING

Introduction

Something powerful happens when you start the day with God. There's a supernatural exchange that takes place. Regardless of the burdens you may be carrying, spending time in the Word and in prayer helps to calm your spirit and refocus your heart. And that allows you to walk through the day with a beautiful strength. Everything may not be perfect, but you will have a godly perspective to guide each step by faith.

Every good day begins with a good morning in the presence of your Father. You may need to wake up earlier or find ways to rearrange your schedule, but choose to have a standing appointment with God before you start the day. And when you do, watch how that sacred space keeps you centered and settled, ready to face whatever the day brings.

Let Me Hear You, God

Father God, some days I wake up feeling ready to take on the world. And other days. . .well, other days I feel ill-equipped to even get out of bed. But either way, God, please shower me with Your love. When I feel capable, content, and motivated, remind me that Your love isn't based on my ability or goodness. When I feel lost, unmotivated, and adrift, I need Your reassurance that You are in control and that Your ways are good. The truth is, Father, no matter how I feel, I trust You. I trust You with my whole self, my entire soul, from the top of my head to the tips of my toes. You created me and know me intimately. Thank You for caring for me so well.

Today, Father, I give You the thoughts that weigh heavily on my mind and heart. I give You the fears I am harboring inside. I ask for Your guidance and wisdom in my decisions, in my relationships, and in every area of my life. I am Yours, Lord. In Jesus' name. Amen.

Let me hear Your loving-kindness in the morning, for I trust in You. Teach me the way I should go for I lift up my soul to You.
PSALM 143:8 NLV

TODAY'S FOCUS POINT

I am listening, Lord.

No Flying Off the Handle

Father God, I don't want to be known as an angry woman. I don't want that to be my legacy. I confess there have been times when my temper got away from me and I responded inappropriately. I've overreacted and caused harm to those I care about the most. And those angry comebacks have boomeranged at me unexpectedly. They've backfired in a spectacular fashion. I own the truth that it was my fault. But I'm ready to let that anger go.

Give me the patience necessary to love others well. Help me choose peace at every turn. Grow the fruit of self-control to maturity in me. My heart's desire is to live a life that glorifies You and blesses others, and flying off the handle doesn't further that worthy pursuit. So today, let scripture be in my heart and on my tongue so every word and action proves my faith authentic. Let calmness permeate every interaction. In Jesus' name. Amen.

Don't be quick to fly off the handle. Anger boomerangs. You can spot a fool by the lumps on his head.
ECCLESIASTES 7:9 MSG

TODAY'S FOCUS POINT

Love is not easily angered.

The Thief of Joy

Father God, I'm exhausted from always comparing myself to others. Why do I look at their best and compare it to my worst every time? When I do, I never come out on top. I'm always falling short of the world's standard. But sometimes I feel like life would just be easier if I were thinner or prettier or taller. Maybe if my hair was different or my skin clearer. Why can't I just love how You made me? And why do I think what's most important are the qualities and features I don't possess?

Today, give me clear eyes to see the good things about me. Let me make peace with who You made me to be. Show me what's valuable in Your eyes, like character and integrity. And remind me that beauty starts from the inside and radiates outward. In Jesus' name. Amen.

Let your true beauty come from your inner personality, not a focus on the external. For lasting beauty comes from a gentle and peaceful spirit, which is precious in God's sight and is much more important than the outward adornment of elaborate hair, jewelry, and fine clothes.

1 PETER 3:3-4 TPT

TODAY'S FOCUS POINT

God made me on purpose.

Being in God's Love

Father God, what a relief to know Your love and mercies are new every morning, because I need them. I need a fresh dose to bolster me throughout the day. What a privilege to be in Your love and reap the beautiful blessings that come from growing in relationship with You. What an honor to be called a child of God, being covered by Your care and compassion every day. You're a faithful Father and I want my life to reflect a commitment to serve You.

No matter what is happening in my day—good or bad—let me feel Your unwavering love in meaningful ways. Let it be what strengthens me when I'm having a hard moment. Let it be what encourages me when I feel hopeless. Let it be what anchors me when the curveballs come. You are my joy and hope, and I'm sticking with You to the end. In Jesus' name. Amen.

GOD's loyal love couldn't have run out, his merciful love couldn't have dried up. They're created new every morning. How great your faithfulness! I'm sticking with GOD (I say it over and over). He's all I've got left.
LAMENTATIONS 3:22–24 MSG

TODAY'S FOCUS POINT

God loves me fully and unconditionally.

Joy in the Morning

Father God, wake me with a heart full of joy each morning. Take away the heaviness of worry and stress that plagued me yesterday, so I am able to feel light as I greet the day. I know pain is part of life, but You are what makes it bearable. God, You're why I can smile when I open my eyes at dawn. You're why I can have hope regardless of my circumstances. You're why I can get out of bed with expectation and excitement.

In those times when sadness lingers and grief hangs on, remind me that these are seasons that will eventually pass. It's Your amazing grace that will remain untouched and unshakable forever. Let that be my source of joy in the morning! No matter what difficulties I'm facing, the holy happiness in my heart doesn't have to be affected. And when I lean on You for help, Your help will be another source of joy. In Jesus' name. Amen.

His wrath, you see, is fleeting, but His grace lasts a lifetime. The deepest pains may linger through the night, but joy greets the soul with the smile of morning.
PSALM 30:5 VOICE

TODAY'S FOCUS POINT

I can have joy no matter what.

Choosing My Attitude

Father God, I'm going to need help with my attitude today! My schedule is filled from morning to night with things I don't want to do—things that often make me cranky. And unless You help me change my perspective so I do everything on my list with a holy mindset, I'm going to make things worse for all involved.

Bless me with Your presence as I keep my eyes focused on You. Help me work as if I'm doing so to glorify Your name. Give me a desire for excellence so I complete each task to the best of my ability. And work on my attitude so I have a servant's heart rather than a selfish one. Today, I will choose to praise You for the opportunity to love others and be Your hands and feet in the world. In Jesus' name. Amen.

Whatever you do [no matter what it is] in word or deed, do everything in the name of the Lord Jesus [and in dependence on Him], giving thanks to God the Father through Him.
COLOSSIANS 3:17 AMP

TODAY'S FOCUS POINT

Today I am serving You.

Divine Dose of Perseverance

Father God, I know my job as a believer is to wait for You to answer my prayers. Sometimes Your answer is an instant response, something I feel right in that moment. But other times—most times—it doesn't match my time frame at all. Help me learn to wait patiently, rather than get frustrated, and trust that You are working on my behalf. Your promises gently remind me that Your heart for me is always good. And Your Word reinforces that You're in control of my life. So give me the ability to rest and trust.

Today, my anxiousness feels a bit overwhelming, and I'm struggling in the waiting. My emotions are complex, and I feel unsettled. Bless me with a divine dose of perseverance as I lay down my stress and worry and let You be God. I've seen You work miracles in my life before, and I know You'll do it again at the right time. My situation is safe in Your mighty hands. In Jesus' name. Amen.

Lord, you know my prayer before I even whisper it. At each and every sunrise you will continue to hear my cry until you answer.
Psalm 88:13 TPT

TODAY'S FOCUS POINT

I can trust God's timing.

The Wrapping of God's Words

Father God, today I want to focus on wrapping Your words into my life. I want to recall every promise You made in scripture for those who believe. I want to soak in the promises I've felt You whisper into my life. I want scripture to run through my head as I step into circumstances that make me feel exposed. And I want reminders of Your goodness to swirl in my heart as I open myself up in honesty to others.

I want to live authentically so others can see my faith. Would You heal any wound that keeps me closed off from those around me? Would You untangle any lies that keep me scared to be real about how I feel? And would You reveal anything in my life that whispers shame into my heart? I'm crying out for You to restore any brokenness. Please repair the places where life has dinged me. And God, replace my hiding tendencies with confidence so I can live in the freedom Jesus came to give. In His name. Amen.

Before the day dawns, I'll be crying out for help
and wrapping your words into my life.
PSALM 119:147 TPT

TODAY'S FOCUS POINT

Vulnerability is beautiful.

God Gives Wisdom

Father God, thank You for offering me the blessing of wisdom when I ask. Sometimes I forget that all I need to do is pray for it. I end up trusting in my own smarts, knocking my head against a wall for fresh ideas. I spend sleepless nights tossing and turning as I search for solutions. And I look for wise counsel here, expecting earthly remedies to be the magical potion to make everything work out. I confess the times I place my hope in other places instead of in You.

So today, I'm boldly asking You to open my mind to Your perfect wisdom. I need the perspective in this situation that only You can provide. I need guidance from the one who understands the intricate details of my circumstances and what I need to know as I navigate them. Fill me with understanding and insight as I prayerfully determine my next steps. I trust You to give me all I need. In Jesus' name. Amen.

*But anyone who needs wisdom should ask God,
whose very nature is to give to everyone without
a second thought, without keeping score. Wisdom
will certainly be given to those who ask.*
JAMES 1:5 CEB

TODAY'S FOCUS POINT

God-given wisdom is the best.

God Is All I Need

Father God, You really are all I need. Forgive me for the times I've misplaced my faith in the offerings of the world. Forgive me for thinking certain people had the answers I needed. I'm sorry for trusting institutions and governments above You. I'm sorry for believing in quick fixes and corporate promises. And I repent of choosing to follow anything that led me from You, of trying to quench my thirsty spirit with earthly antidotes. I see my mistakes.

Let today mark the change in my heart. In my failures, I only need Your help and restoration to move forward. I've learned the hard way that You're the answer to every need I have. I'm tired of looking in all the wrong places for hope. I trust You, Father. In every situation, Your presence is what protects me. Your anointing is what empowers my faith to believe in You above all else. In Jesus' name. Amen.

Lord, so many times I fail; I fall into disgrace. But when I trust in you, I have a strong and glorious presence protecting and anointing me. Forever you're all I need!
PSALM 73:26 TPT

TODAY'S FOCUS POINT

God is my everything.

God Will Light the Dark Path

Father God, sometimes I feel so lost in life. I don't always know the next right step for me. And when I think I see the endgame clearly, I don't always know which path to take to get me there. I want to follow Your leading, but how can I know it's You I'm hearing? So I end up paralyzed, unable to move forward in confidence.

Because scripture says Your words will illuminate even the darkest path, direct me to the perfect scripture. Show me passages in the Bible that will connect with my confused heart and clearly direct my decisions. Interrupt my day. Father, get my attention. Drive my desire to open Your holy Word to find wisdom and discernment. Let it fill me with inspiration. I want only what You want for me. Nothing else. In Jesus' name. Amen.

By your words I can see where I'm going; they throw a beam of light on my dark path. I've committed myself and I'll never turn back from living by your righteous order. Everything's falling apart on me, GOD; put me together again with your Word.
PSALM 119:105–107 MSG

TODAY'S FOCUS POINT

What does God want for me?

The Pursuit of Compassionate Living

Father God, because You are compassionate, I can be too. Because You came for the brokenhearted, You give me the ability to love them fiercely as well. And since You love me with a steadfast love, I am able to rise above my earthly feelings and boldly love others, even when it's difficult. Through faith, I can forgive those I deem unforgivable. When You asked us to be kind and helpful, You meant for us to live that way toward everyone.

Forgive me for every judgment I've passed. I'm sorry for my dismissive attitude toward the broken. I confess the times I've lacked compassion when I should have had tons of it. But starting today, my heart's desire is to be Your hands and feet to a hurting world. Show me how to love others unconditionally. Help me release offenses and promote understanding. Let my mission to be kindhearted succeed as I trust You to fill me with endless amounts of kindness. In Jesus' name. Amen.

Be kind and helpful to one another, tender-hearted [compassionate, understanding], forgiving one another [readily and freely], just as God in Christ also forgave you.
EPHESIANS 4:32 AMP

TODAY'S FOCUS POINT

Who needs compassion today?

Confident Faith

Father God, what I need right now is radical trust in Your promises. There are so many moving parts in my life, and I can't seem to believe that everything will work out for the best. When I think about it all, I only see terrible outcomes and endings. And I feel too weak to try to work it out. God, I need You to strengthen me and still my anxious heart.

Grow steadfast confidence in me. Let me feel a boldness rise up like never before. Help me have radical trust in Your sovereignty and goodness. And let me have a front row seat as You divinely orchestrate the loose ends in my life. I've seen You bring beauty from ashes, and I know You can do it again. I love You, Father. I humbly accept the invitation to live in Your will and ways, following the path You've determined for me to walk. In Jesus' name. Amen.

We are confident that God is able to orchestrate everything to work toward something good and beautiful when we love Him and accept His invitation to live according to His plan.
ROMANS 8:28 VOICE

TODAY'S FOCUS POINT

Trust God's plan.

When I'm Afraid to Trust God

Father God, help me feel safe enough to trust You. I've faced so much betrayal in my life that I struggle to think anyone would have my best in mind. My days are filled with doubt and hypervigilance. And honestly, I'm tired. Depending only on myself is exhausting because I'm never able to let my guard down. But I know part of faith means trusting You with my heart.

Help me break down the walls and embrace the fullness of Your love. Today, give me courage to be open and honest with You about what I'm feeling. Whether I'm struggling in relationships, battling with my health, or stressed trying to make ends meet, remind me that You want to hear it all. You know everything anyway. I don't want to be a lukewarm believer. Instead, I want to be all in and create a robust relationship with You that has a firm foundation of trust and faith. In Jesus' name. Amen.

Have faith in Him in all circumstances,
dear people. Open up your heart to Him;
the True God shelters us in His arms.
PSALM 62:8 VOICE

TODAY'S FOCUS POINT

God is always faithful.

The Need for Discernment

Father God, I've come to a crossroads. Both roads look promising even though they lead in different directions. But I feel uncertain about the best one to take in this situation. As I begin my day in prayer, I'm asking for Your divine discernment to be my guide. Help me be confident as I make important decisions.

I feel like I know the difference between right and wrong. As a believer, I have invested time in Your Word. I've sought Your wisdom and guidance through prayer countless times in my life. And I'm connected to a God-fearing community. But in this circumstance, I want clarity. This feels weighty, and I need Your discernment before taking my next step. In Jesus' name. Amen.

But solid food is for the mature, whose spiritual senses perceive heavenly matters. And they have been adequately trained by what they've experienced to emerge with understanding of the difference between what is truly excellent and what is evil and harmful.
HEBREWS 5:14 TPT

TODAY'S FOCUS POINT

God's discernment is my pursuit.

When Distractions Usurp Faith

Father God, help me stay focused on Your wisdom above all else because the distractions of the world cause me to make snap decisions. When I feel rushed, I don't think through the details. I don't look at the natural consequences I might face. And rather than take my issues to You, I allow worldly things to usurp my faith. I make choices with a divided heart when I should be looking to You alone. Forgive me.

Instead, let me meditate on Your Word and find the wisdom necessary to take the right steps without being pulled in different directions. Let that wisdom remind me that Your way is the way of truth and life. Your plans for me are well thought out and intentional. Your will and timing are perfect. As I choose to look to You alone each day, no earthly distraction can interfere in my pursuit to live righteously and glorify Your name. In Jesus' name. Amen.

I ponder every morsel of wisdom from you, I attentively watch how you've done it. I relish everything you've told me of life, I won't forget a word of it.
PSALM 119:15–16 MSG

TODAY'S FOCUS POINT

Distractions take my eyes off God.

My Faith Pleases God

Father God, Your Word says that I cannot please You without faith. I need to believe not only that You are alive but also that You're active in my life. While my salvation is secure because I'm a believer, I confess that I still struggle with doubt sometimes. It's hard to believe that You will come through because my ears can't hear You confirm it. There are times I want You seated in front of me so I can see Your expression and feel Your affirming hugs. But faith is believing without those, and I need Your help.

With all my heart, I want the words I say and the thoughts I think to please You every day. I want my actions to delight Your heart in fresh ways. I want to begin my conversation with You before my feet hit the floor in the morning. And I want prayers to be my last waking act. See my faith—even when it's messy—and count me as righteous in Your eyes. In Jesus' name. Amen.

It's impossible to please God apart from faith.
And why? Because anyone who wants to approach
God must believe both that he exists and that he
cares enough to respond to those who seek him.
HEBREWS 11:6 MSG

TODAY'S FOCUS POINT

Make my faith unshakable.

God Saves Me from Fear

Father God, I know Your Word tells me not to be afraid over 350 times. In its pages, You commanded countless people to fear not. You must have known it would be a big deal. For me, fear follows relentlessly, and it steals my peace and takes my joy. Thank You for the reminder once again that when I require help, all I need to do is ask. Rather than let worry or anxiety take root, my job is to flex my faith.

So hear me, Father! My circumstances feel overwhelming, and I'm racked with fear of what may come next. Save me today, Lord. Lift me out of the what-ifs and settle my heart. Let me feel Your love surround me on all sides. Fortify me with Your strength. Fill me with courage and confidence. And make me fearless, knowing my Father always has my back. In Jesus' name. Amen.

When I needed the Lord, I looked for Him; I called out to Him, and He heard me and responded. He came and rescued me from everything that made me so afraid.
PSALM 34:4 VOICE

TODAY'S FOCUS POINT

God makes me strong and courageous.

Being Quick to Forgive

Father God, why is forgiving so difficult for me? I should be quick to do it, especially when I think of how You forgave me in my wretchedness. Letting go of offenses should be second nature. But it's a struggle.

Help me become a woman who lives in the freedom that Jesus came to give. I don't want to be hindered by unforgiveness. While You don't want me to be a doormat, Your command is for me to extend grace every time. I may need to create boundaries for toxic people, but I can still forgive. I may need to end relationships that are unhealthy, but I don't have to collect offenses. Thank You for forgiving my trespasses. Now let me be quick to do the same for others—not for their sake, but for mine. And because it's what You've commanded for those who love You. In Jesus' name. Amen.

Then Peter said to Jesus, "Lord, how many times should I forgive my brother or sister who sins against me? Should I forgive as many as seven times?" Jesus said, "Not just seven times, but rather as many as seventy-seven times."
MATTHEW 18:21-22 CEB

TODAY'S FOCUS POINT

I will extend grace to others.

Showing Kindness to Enemies

Father God, I'll be honest. Sometimes I wish You asked easier things of me. Living a righteous life takes dedication and self-lessness that often seems unattainable. There are some commands that feel more natural to me. Some fruits of the Spirit are almost second nature. But knowing You want me to show radical kindness to those who despise me feels impossible. Without Your help, I will fail every time.

I know what it feels like to harbor bitterness, and I also know what it feels like to extend compassion. The difference is night and day. So give me Your heart for kindness. Fill me with a spirit of benevolence. Teach me how to bless those who curse me and pray for the ones who harass me. And give me a servant's heart to show love to the unlovable. In Jesus' name. Amen.

"But I say to you who hear, love your enemies and do something wonderful for them in return for their hatred. When someone curses you, bless that person in return. When others mistreat and harass you, accept it as your mission to pray for them. To those who despise you, continue to serve them and minister to them."
LUKE 6:27–29 TPT

TODAY'S FOCUS POINT

Choosing to be kind in every circumstance.

The Best Kind of Friendship

Father God, bring me friends who passionately love You. Surround me with women who seek Your face as they pursue righteous living. I want to be in community with others who will hold me accountable to Your standards in every circumstance. We are on this adventure of faith together, and part of loving means challenging one another when necessary. It's not sitting in the judgment seat, because that's reserved for You only. But instead, it's caring enough to sharpen character from a place of genuine care and concern.

There is something special about these close relationships. There's a feeling of security that radiates from them, especially knowing our foundation of faith is rooted together. Father, let that be what strengthens our friendship and tightens our bond. I'm excited for the community You will bring my way at the right time. Prepare me for the blessing of it! And let me be the kind of friend who brings blessings in return. In Jesus' name. Amen.

In the same way that iron sharpens iron,
a person sharpens the character of his friend.
PROVERBS 27:17 VOICE

TODAY'S FOCUS POINT

Pray for the gift of faith-filled friends.

Choosing Words Wisely

Father God, help me choose my words wisely. Give me discernment so I am able to speak with the perfect combination of truth and love. The last thing I'd want to do is harm others because of something I shared. Help me distinguish between what can be made public and what should remain private. And keep me from being interested in the lies and gossip others carelessly share with anyone who will listen. I want to be different than that.

Starting today, give me the courage to stand up for what's right. Give me confidence to be a bold advocate for kind and generous words—both the ones I speak and the ones spoken to me. Scripture says that when we are mindful of what we say, it will create a good, long life. Help me embrace this truth and teach it to those who will listen. In Jesus' name. Amen.

If you love life and want to live a good, long time, take care with the things you say. Don't lie or spread gossip or talk about improper things. Walk away from the evil things of the world, and always seek peace and pursue it.
PSALM 34:12–14 VOICE

TODAY'S FOCUS POINT

Let my words bring life.

The Beautiful Pursuit of Harmony

Father God, the world is in such chaos right now. We see wars and hear rumors of more. People become emboldened as they sit behind a keyboard and type out the meanest things on social media. Our politicians argue incessantly, which sets the tone for the country. What we lack right now is peace.

I'm grateful that regardless of what's going on, I can create my own bubble of joy when I follow Your ways. Help me stay in that beautiful space with You today! I am choosing to release offenses and bless those who hate me. I'm choosing to laugh with the happy and cry with the brokenhearted. I want to be humble. I don't want to discriminate when it comes to friends. My heart's desire is to get along with others whenever possible. Please bring this plan to fruition and let me be an agent of peace wherever I go. In Jesus' name. Amen.

*Bless your enemies; no cursing under your breath.
Laugh with your happy friends when they're
happy; share tears when they're down. Get along
with each other; don't be stuck-up. Make friends
with nobodies; don't be the great somebody.*
Romans 12:14–16 msg

TODAY'S FOCUS POINT

Be a peacemaker whenever possible.

When the Waiting Is Hard

Father God, there are few things harder for me than waiting. When I have an idea, I want to execute it immediately. When I'm struggling with a decision, I want to make up my mind right then and there. When a relationship feels unstable, I want resolution to happen quickly. When my finances are in trouble, I crave instant solutions. And when I go to You in prayer for guidance, I desperately want an answer within the hour.

When my spirit gets stirred up by fear, would You calm my anxious heart? It's this fear that drives me to impatience. Help me relinquish control and trust that You are working in each situation. The tighter I hold on to the stress, the more demanding I become. I get annoyed and irritated easily. But I know trusting You instead will strengthen me. It will give me the right perspective as I wait for You to inform or intervene. I'll have the peace I need, knowing You're working all things out. In Jesus' name. Amen.

But those who trust in the Eternal One will regain their strength. They will soar on wings as eagles. They will run—never winded, never weary. They will walk—never tired, never faint.
ISAIAH 40:31 VOICE

TODAY'S FOCUS POINT

Trusting God strengthens me to wait.

Hope Will Never Fail

Father God, sometimes I feel so hopeless that life won't get any better. It seems everywhere I turn the news is hard to swallow. I see broken relationships and deterioration of health. I'm watching financial ruin play out. I see sadness and grief in those I love. And it breaks my heart and discourages me. That is, when I focus my attention on the world.

But what a blessing to know that the Holy Spirit will make good on Your promise to satisfy my deepest needs. I can have hope because I have You. It's because You love me so deeply that I don't have to live in despair. Even if the circumstances around me remain the same, I can live with an unfailing hope that You will come through in the end. You will sustain me through every difficult moment. You will meet every need—spoken and unspoken. You will fill me with joy and peace. And through You, I will live a hope-filled life knowing my eternity is secure. Help me share that hope with the brokenhearted. In Jesus' name. Amen.

And hope will never fail to satisfy our deepest need because the Holy Spirit that was given to us has flooded our hearts with God's love.
ROMANS 5:5 VOICE

TODAY'S FOCUS POINT

There is always hope with God.

The Lies That Create Insecurity

Father God, I know You made me on purpose and for a purpose. I know You took time thinking me up, choosing everything from my hair color to when I'd arrive on the kingdom calendar. Your Word says You knit me together in my mother's womb, so I am an intentional creation. I'm not a mistake. I'm not unwanted. But there are times when the message I hear the loudest is the one saying the complete opposite.

Help me focus on the truth that I am loved rather than listen to the enemy, who wants to destroy my sense of value. When I'm battling insecurity, certain I'm not good enough, remind me that Jesus came for me. The enemy wants to discourage, but You promise to encourage me as I rest in You. Let me see myself through Your eyes. Fill my heart to overflowing with an understanding of Your acceptance. And let me live today full of joy because I know I am the daughter of the King. In Jesus' name. Amen.

The thief comes only in order to steal and kill and destroy. I came that they may have and enjoy life, and have it in abundance (to the full, till it overflows).

JOHN 10:10 AMPC

TODAY'S FOCUS POINT

I'm created on purpose for a purpose.

Uncovering Jealousy

Father God, would You help me find contentment in who You created me to be? Help me be satisfied with my life and the journey I'm on. Let me be pleased with where I live and the job I have. Let me be happy with the community that surrounds me. While I know it's good to strive for excellence, pushing with the wrong motives will certainly tangle me up in knots of discontent. I want to love and appreciate the life I have right now, unwilling to compare it to the life anyone else is living. I know if my heart is unsettled, it's a good indication that there's something hiding under the surface.

God, in Your infinite wisdom, please heal any broken places in me. Uncover what causes jealousy so we can work through it together. Don't leave me to my own devices. It's only getting me deeper into selfishness and pity. Today, open my eyes to see every blessing in my life. Give me a heart of gratitude. And make me content and fulfilled in You. In Jesus' name. Amen.

So wherever jealousy and selfishness are uncovered, you will also find many troubles and every kind of meanness.
JAMES 3:16 TPT

TODAY'S FOCUS POINT

Adopt an attitude of gratitude.

Loving Deeply and Fully

Father God, Your love is perfect. It's complete. And I'm so grateful I didn't have to earn it. Knowing there's nothing that could make You love me any *more* or any *less* brings comfort. It reminds me that Your love is unconditional. What's more, it's the purest kind of love that can't be replicated anywhere else.

As I think about it, I can recall feeling Your love in the hard moments I've faced. I've felt it in times of celebration. I can recall the ways You've demonstrated compassion when I needed it the most. And I've witnessed Your love in the lives of others. Let me be a lover of people in the same ways. Give me a heart for my community and help me share with others in meaningful ways. Today, let me love others deeply and fully so they are blessed by You, through me. In Jesus' name. Amen.

So I give you a new command: Love each other deeply and fully. Remember the ways that I have loved you, and demonstrate your love for others in those same ways. Everyone will know you as My followers if you demonstrate your love to others.

JOHN 13:34-35 VOICE

TODAY'S FOCUS POINT

How can I demonstrate love today?

Why Motivation Matters

Father God, when I'm struggling with motivation, remind me to look to You for help. Whether I'm trying to eat healthier or taking a class that's super difficult or trying to be more present during family times—whatever it may be, God, please partner with me and provide the grit to persevere with passion and purpose. It's hard for me to stay engaged when I'm trying to make changes in my life, and I need You to help me stand firm in my commitments.

Today, I am determined to be confident as I pursue good things. It's important that I follow through, especially knowing others are watching. Endurance will bless me, but it will also bless and encourage those lacking their own determination. Fortitude is contagious! And Your help is precious. In Jesus' name. Amen.

So now, beloved ones, stand firm, stable, and enduring.
Live your lives with an unshakable confidence. We know
that we prosper and excel in every season by serving
the Lord, because we are assured that our union with the
Lord makes our labor productive with fruit that endures.
1 CORINTHIANS 15:58 TPT

TODAY'S FOCUS POINT

My motivation to change is unshakable.

Empowered to Obey

Father God, can I be honest? There are times when Your commands feel too lofty. They just feel too big, like something only a Moses or an Abraham could do. I often feel unqualified to walk them out. When I think back to my sinful past (and current struggles with sin), I can't see a way that I can obediently follow what You ask. So rather than feel like a failure over and over again, I sometimes just opt out. I don't even try.

Scripture says Your love can change that kind of mindset. It tells me that choosing to embrace Your love will empower me to obey. And so today, I'm asking You to make that happen in my life. Let me be so aware of Your love that it transforms my heart. Open my eyes to see the ways Your love is demonstrated in my circumstances, making it impossible not to follow Your command with fervor. My heart's desire is to glorify You with how I live my life, but I can't do it without Your divine intervention. Be with me today and inspire me to please You with each choice I make. In Jesus' name. Amen.

"Loving me empowers you to obey my commands."
JOHN 14:15 TPT

TODAY'S FOCUS POINT

God's love empowers me to obey.

Whose Approval Do You Want?

Father God, today the only approval I want is Yours. Too often, I find myself working to please others. I want my parents to think I make good choices. I want my kids to see an unflustered mom. I want my friends to see a thoughtful person. I want my employer to see a hardworking team member. I want my husband to see a wife who can do it all. And to be honest, I'm exhausted and bitter.

The goal for me, starting now, is to please You with how I live my life. (And by doing so, others may be blessed too.) All I need is Your approval to make me feel valued. This will be difficult, I know. So help me keep my eyes on You, following Your will and ways. Let my pursuit to delight You be what drives my day. In Jesus' name. Amen.

For they loved the approval and the praise and the glory that come from men [instead of and] more than the glory that comes from God. [They valued their credit with men more than their credit with God.]
JOHN 12:43 AMPC

TODAY'S FOCUS POINT

My desire is to please God.

The Desperate Need for Kindness

Father God, with our nation and the world in chaos, let me be a ray of light in the lives of those I meet. Let me choose to be kind and generous at every turn, blessing others in meaningful ways. There is always a need for compassion, and I want to be one who gives it in abundance. Would You fill my heart to overflowing? And from that, show me where to pour it out to the lost and broken. Use me to be Your hands and feet in the world. Guide me to the places where I can love those who need it the most. Give me the right words at the right time to speak encouragement.

Lord, please also bring Your kindness into my life in fresh ways. Today, I could use reminders that I am loved and valued. Sometimes life feels so heavy, and a generous word lifts my spirit. Just as I want to share thoughtfulness, I would love to have it shared with me. I could really use it right now. Thank You for hearing my pleas. In Jesus' name. Amen.

Pleasant words are like a honeycomb, sweet and
delightful to the soul and healing to the body.
PROVERBS 16:24 AMP

TODAY'S FOCUS POINT

Choose to be kind whenever possible.

The Goal to Trust

Father God, I've seen the ways You've blessed me with Your loving hands in the past. I've watched You show up in hopeless situations for those I love. Your faithfulness is unmatched in all the world! Knowing this, it's frustrating for me when my initial reaction is to manage things without Your guidance. I confess my struggle with doubt at times, and I'm asking You to strengthen my faith in response.

My goal for today is to trust You with all my heart. I'm going to stand in my belief that You will come through. I know You'll guide me as I make decisions and You'll lead me as I purpose to follow Your will for my day. God, I want to trust You fully, without any hesitation. Give me the ability to flex my faith regardless of what comes my way. In Jesus' name. Amen.

Trust in the Lord completely, and do not rely on your own opinions. With all your heart rely on him to guide you, and he will lead you in every decision you make. Become intimate with him in whatever you do, and he will lead you wherever you go.
PROVERBS 3:5-6 TPT

TODAY'S FOCUS POINT

I can trust God with everything!

When I'm Not Content

Father God, my heart is so full today knowing I am Your child. Being in Your family—that's my safe place. It's where I feel loved and valued. Being Your beloved is where I anchor my identity. You are a good, good Father, and I'm so thankful to have been chosen.

But on those days when I'm down and struggling, remind me I can find much-needed contentment in the depths of Your love. Help me be quick to turn back to You rather than sit in my own pity party. Bless me with a heavenly perspective that shifts my focus off me and my problems and puts it on the good things at work through Your capable hands. Lift my eyes to see You! In Jesus' name. Amen.

So if you're serious about living this new resurrection life with Christ, act like it. Pursue the things over which Christ presides. Don't shuffle along, eyes to the ground, absorbed with the things right in front of you. Look up, and be alert to what is going on around Christ—that's where the action is. See things from his perspective.

COLOSSIANS 3:1–2 MSG

TODAY'S FOCUS POINT

Contentment starts with eyes on God.

When I Feel Dissatisfied

Father God, there are days when my attention focuses on all I do not have. I see others with thriving marriages, but mine is not. I look at their homes and wardrobes, realizing I cannot compete. I watch where they vacation, when I haven't taken one in years. I compare the successes of my husband and kids to others, and we always fall short. And when I should be content with every blessing in my life—and there are plenty—I'm trying to measure up instead.

Lord, as I go about my day, help me become aware of the situations that make me feel dissatisfied. Get my attention when I begin to compare or envy. I want the Holy Spirit to nudge me when my mind begins to wander into restlessness. Today, empower me to guard my heart against greed and instead find comfort in You. In Jesus' name. Amen.

Speaking to the people, Jesus continued, "Be alert and guard your heart from greed and from always wishing for what you don't have. For your life can never be measured by the amount of things you possess."
LUKE 12:15 TPT

TODAY'S FOCUS POINT

I will guard my heart against comparison.

Inspired with Wisdom

Father God, forgive me for the times I've thought myself wiser than You. Deep down I know I'm not. Sometimes I just forget to include You in my decisions. Or I think it's a small issue that doesn't require Your input. Or I feel fully equipped to manage alone, even though You want to be part of that too. And other times, I know what I'm choosing doesn't glorify You and just want what I want. I'm sorry for leaving You out of the equation.

I'm going to seek You for wisdom every day and in every way. I'm going to dig into the Bible and explore Your words. I'm going to take a breath before making decisions so I can respond in faith and not in fear. I will follow You, Lord, with all my heart. Your wisdom leads to life every time. In Jesus' name. Amen.

Carefully consider all that I've taught you, and may our Lord inspire you with wisdom and revelation in everything you say and do.

2 TIMOTHY 2:7 TPT

TODAY'S FOCUS POINT

Ask God for guidance in decisions.

Showing Compassion to All

Father God, Your Word tells me to show all people compassion. Not just the ones who are easy to love. Not only those who follow You. And not just the people who are like me. You say I'm to have mercy on everyone. I want to obey, but I'm going to need Your help.

The truth is that it's hard to have mercy on those who have hurt me. Sometimes I feel uncomfortable interacting with people who have different lives and beliefs than me. But today, I'm going to step out of my comfort zone and follow Your command. I'm going to show compassion to everyone I see. It may be speaking a kind word, lending a helping hand, or giving financial support. But my heart is open and so are my eyes. Use me, Lord! In Jesus' name. Amen.

Here is what the Eternal, Commander of heavenly armies, has to say: "Dispense true justice, have mercy on others, and show all people compassion. Do not take advantage of those who have lost a spouse or a parent, or those who are outsiders or poor. Don't purpose to do evil toward your fellow Israelites."
ZECHARIAH 7:9–10 VOICE

TODAY'S FOCUS POINT

Compassion toward all is a command.

The Beauty of Perseverance

Father God, thank You for including stories in the Bible of people who persevered under pressure. When I'm really struggling, spending time reading their accounts always encourages me to stay the course. To know what Job endured and Joseph walked through is powerful. To read about Hannah praying relentlessly for a baby and Noah building the ark while being criticized is inspiring. Just to understand the faith it took to stand strong in their difficult circumstances bolsters my own faith to do the same in mine.

Create in me an unshakable character of perseverance. Never let the troubles of each day wear me down or take me out of the game altogether, because I possess a faith that is unwavering. My heart is full of gratitude for those who have endured under hardship. Be it people from the Bible or people in my own community, their legacy lives on in me. In Jesus' name. Amen.

Look, we bless and honor the memory of those who persevered under hardship. Remember how Job endured and how the Lord orchestrated the triumph of his final circumstances as a grand display of His mercy and compassion.
JAMES 5:11 VOICE

TODAY'S FOCUS POINT

Faith enables me to persevere.

The Gift of Compassion

Father God, I know Your compassion for me is weighty because I feel it in the most amazing ways. Thank You for showing me how loved I am, especially when I'm certain I'm unlovable. Thank You for bringing help and hope in Your perfect time. And thank You for choosing me to be Your beloved. It's because of this I'm able to extend mercy and kindness toward those around me.

Today, please give me the ability to love others in the beautiful ways You love me. Let me be humble rather than haughty, remembering I'm not their savior. Give me a gentle understanding of what others are going through so I can help. And from the overflow of holy compassion You've shown me, let me bless those who need it the most. In Jesus' name. Amen.

You are always and dearly loved by God! So robe yourself with virtues of God, since you have been divinely chosen to be holy. Be merciful as you endeavor to understand others, and be compassionate, showing kindness toward all. Be gentle and humble, unoffendable in your patience with others.
COLOSSIANS 3:12 TPT

TODAY'S FOCUS POINT

Treat others with holy compassion.

Stand Unmoved

Father God, I confess my battle with worry. It's overwhelming at times, and unsettling—especially because I know You are God! I know You are sovereign! I have experienced Your goodness in the valleys. I've seen You come through when my circumstances looked hopeless. But still, my faith wavers from time to time.

Lord, strengthen me. Grow my faith muscle so I can stand unmoved as I patiently wait for Your hand to move in my sight line. And when I can't see You, remind me that You're always working on my behalf. There's no circumstance You're unaware of. There's no anxiety You don't see. There's no concern of mine You miss. Lord, today I am choosing to trust in Your provision and power. In Jesus' name. Amen.

> *"If God gives such attention to the appearance of wildflowers—most of which are never even seen— don't you think he'll attend to you, take pride in you, do his best for you? What I'm trying to do here is to get you to relax, to not be so preoccupied with getting, so you can respond to God's giving."*
> MATTHEW 6:30–31 MSG

TODAY'S FOCUS POINT

God will always provide for me.

God Is Your Fear Buster

Father God, today's scripture makes an interesting point I want to meditate on. It tells me that it's Your presence that will bring comfort to my fearful soul. When I panic, it's remembering You're with me that will bring a calm to my anxious heart. When I'm afraid, it's knowing You're my God that will strengthen me to overcome the things that scare me.

Today, Lord, will You help me stand up to my Goliaths? Will You steady my shaky hands and quiet my knocking knees as I rise up in faith? Keep Your firm grip on me as I navigate the situations that freak me out. I don't want to cower any longer. Instead, I am choosing to believe deep in my heart that You are my constant companion and fear buster. With You by my side, I am safe and intrepid. In Jesus' name. Amen.

"Don't panic. I'm with you. There's no need to fear
for I'm your God. I'll give you strength. I'll help you.
I'll hold you steady, keep a firm grip on you."
Isaiah 41:10 MSG

TODAY'S FOCUS POINT

God's consistent presence cures my fear.

The Power of Worship

Father God, hear my prayers of praise for who You are and all the wonders You've done in my life. Let my attitude of gratitude delight Your heart and reveal my deep appreciation for Your mighty hand. Let my thankfulness ring in the heavens as I worship You, the God of creation, with my life. And keep my imperfect words and flawed actions from diminishing the authenticity of my admiration for Your kingship. I give You every breath of praise in my lungs.

Thank You for the times You've closed the wrong doors and opened the right ones. Thank You for saving me from bad decisions. Thank You for healing my broken heart and restoring hope in the future. And thank You for surrounding me with Your continual presence today and every day, for it brings me comfort. In Jesus' name. Amen.

Come on, everyone! Let's sing for joy to the Lord! Let's shout our loudest praises to our God who saved us! Everyone come meet his face with a thankful heart. Don't hold back your praises; make him great by your shouts of joy! For the Lord is the greatest of all, King-God over all other gods!
PSALM 95:1-3 TPT

TODAY'S FOCUS POINT

Praising God is a privilege.

Wisdom through Song

Father God, Your words are like a song in my heart. They are a melody to my soul. And as I meditate on them today, let them be what guides me to walk in Your wisdom. Let them live within me richly so they become a part of my DNA and provide divine discernment. My heart desires to know Your plan for my life—Your will and ways—because You're my compass.

It feels a little weird to sing to You like this, but hear my voice rise up in prayers for Your support. Listen to my spirit singing for more of Your presence in my day as I obey Your leading. Let my gratitude reach to the heavens, praising You for helping me find the right path to follow. And let me thrive in a community of believers who will seek and share truth, helping one another live right and pleasing lives in Your name. In Jesus' name. Amen.

The word of Christ must live in you richly. Teach and warn each other with all wisdom by singing psalms, hymns, and spiritual songs. Sing to God with gratitude in your hearts.
COLOSSIANS 3:16 CEB

TODAY'S FOCUS POINT

Put my favorite scriptures to song.

It Takes Strength to Be Humble

Father God, I can think of countless times I was certain my way was right. I've picked fights to get my way. I've thought myself too wise, railroading others in hurtful ways. And while I am an educated woman with tons of hard-won wisdom under my belt, I confess the times I put the value of my knowledge above others—above You. It was a prideful mistake, and I'm sorry for being so presumptuous.

Create in me a humble heart, Lord. Take away any haughty attitude that makes me think I am better than those around me. I want to be meek, while understanding that doesn't mean I am weak. True humility takes strength and I'm asking for that. Let me be quick to listen to the ideas and opinions of others. Let me always see Your wisdom above all else. And give me a heart for collaboration and community. They work together beautifully. In Jesus' name. Amen.

When you act with presumption, convinced that you're right, don't be surprised if you fall flat on your face! But humility leads to wisdom.
PROVERBS 11:2 TPT

TODAY'S FOCUS POINT

Be open to the ideas of others.

A Walk in Worship

Father God, it's so amazing to realize that You knew me before I even took a breath of air. You formed me in my mother's womb. You knitted me together with foreknowledge of the life You chose for me to follow. All throughout my days, You have been my constant support. Under Your care, I have journeyed through valleys and mountaintop experiences and have come out stronger and wiser. You've saved me. Healed me. Restored me. And I stand here today a miracle in so many ways.

Every success I have earned is thanks to Your guidance. Every achievement is attributed to Your mighty love. Any kindness and generosity I'm able to share is because of my transformed heart. My ability to extend grace is because You first forgave me. Today, let me walk in worship as I meditate on Your goodness! In Jesus' name. Amen.

It was you who supported me from the day I was born, loving me, helping me through my life's journey. You've made me into a miracle; no wonder I trust you and praise you forever! Many marvel at my success, but I know it is all because of you, my mighty protector!

PSALM 71:6–7 TPT

TODAY'S FOCUS POINT

Every good thing comes from God.

Victory Mindset

Father God, today I feel weak in battle. I'm overwhelmed because there are too many hard things to navigate, and my spirit is unsettled. From relationship woes to financial concerns to my deep insecurities, I lack the confidence to advocate for my needs. I lack the courage to speak up and say what needs to be said. Will You fill me with power so I can stand in strength and trust You?

The world is always ready to jump in with solutions, trying to take my eyes off You. But I've been down that road countless times, and it offers no true solution to the hardships I face. So Lord, help me stand victorious because in You the battle is already won. Rather than let self-doubt win, I will secure my hope in Your mighty hand. In Jesus' name. Amen.

Through your glorious name and your awesome power, we can push through to any victory and defeat every enemy. For I will not trust in the weapons of the world; I know they will never save me. Only you will be our Savior from all our enemies. All those who hate us you have brought to shame.

PSALM 44:5–7 TPT

TODAY'S FOCUS POINT

Victory doesn't come from the world.

How Hearing Grows Faith

Father God, open my ears to hear, and command my attention to listen for Your divine words in sermons, worship music, and the testimonies of others. If there is a message for me, make it known. Let it be a game changer for my heart as it brings truth and encouragement to my parched soul. I know that faith grows from hearing messages of Your goodness. Let me not mindlessly tune out the nuggets of wisdom You have for me.

In the mornings, speak to me through my quiet time with You. Let me wake up ready to meet with my Father. In the evenings, let me recall the wisdom I received throughout the day. Let me meditate on the right things. And as we talk in between, let my faith grow because of meaningful moments and divine interactions. Keep my ear turned toward You always, Lord. Boldly speak so I hear You and am blessed by it. In Jesus' name. Amen.

So faith comes from hearing [what is told],
and what is heard comes by the [preaching
of the] message concerning Christ.
ROMANS 10:17 AMP

TODAY'S FOCUS POINT

Look and listen for God's wisdom.

God's Wisdom above Mine

Father God, help me consistently make good choices. Give me conviction in the decisions I make so I can be assured they not only benefit me but also glorify You. Maybe that means I slow down and take a breath rather than make rash rulings. The truth is that for so long I've been comfortable relying on myself to figure things out. I figured I had enough life experience under my belt and could discern right from wrong without any outside help. But scripture tells me that's wrong.

Teach me to walk in Your wisdom instead of my own. Today, train me to lean on You for understanding. Help me remember to always trust in Your knowledge and insight because it's flawless. And let my confidence grow daily, allowing me to make the best choices because my mind and heart are filled with Your divine inspiration. Lord, I don't want to be a fool. I want to be faithful. In Jesus' name. Amen.

He who leans on, trusts in, and is confident of his own mind and heart is a [self-confident] fool, but he who walks in skillful and godly Wisdom shall be delivered.
PROVERBS 28:26 AMPC

TODAY'S FOCUS POINT

Godly wisdom trumps my wisdom.

Strength for the Victory

Father God, I confess that I've often relied on the weapons and wisdom of the world. The world is quick to offer solutions that feel good. It sells easy fixes. But in the end, I'm left with nothing more than compounded frustration and heartache. What the world offers me will never be a true remedy because it's incapable of matching what You generously offer.

Lord, thank You for filling me with Your strength today. It's why I can stand strong when my relationships get messy. It's why I can stay cool when my health or finances take a turn for the worse. And it's through Your strength alone that I will always find my miracle-deliverance. You're the one who gives me much-needed victory over the battles I face. As I walk into my day, let Your power and might course through my veins, securing my hope in You over anything else. In Jesus' name. Amen.

Some find their strength in their weapons and wisdom, but my miracle-deliverance can never be won by men. Our boast is in Yahweh our God, who makes us strong and gives us victory!

PSALM 20:7 TPT

TODAY'S FOCUS POINT

God's strength leads to victory.

When You Need Perseverance

Father God, I need grit and grace to stay strong in this battle. Everything in me wants to curl up in a ball and hide away. I want to walk out of this stressful situation rather than stay engaged and work at resolution. And I'm feeling weak in my resolve to do the right thing. Honestly, I just want relief, and I'm craving that change in real time. Please intervene today and give me an infusion of faith so I can hang on.

My heart's desire is to be a woman of perseverance! Regardless of the battle, let my heart be steadfast as I focus on You. Keep my eyes open with wisdom and discernment for what comes next. Help me cling to my convictions, trusting they will steady me through the process. Give me unbendable resolve to stay the course with You at the helm. And let me love big so I don't let any stress or worry come out at those I care about. I know I can stay strong through You! In Jesus' name. Amen.

Keep your eyes open, hold tight to your convictions, give it all you've got, be resolute, and love without stopping.
1 CORINTHIANS 16:13–14 MSG

TODAY'S FOCUS POINT

In faith, I can persevere to the end.

When You're Craving Confidence

Father God, help me be confident in Your provision and care, especially when I'm hit with unsettling news. I don't need to stress out or worry about the future because You are already there. I don't have to be concerned about horrible outcomes and endings, for You're with me through the valleys and mountaintop experiences. I don't need to panic, because You promise to keep me safe and sound, protected in Your loving care.

Today I'm asking for Your precious reassurance to wash over me. I am desperate for powerful reminders that You've got me no matter what. When things around me feel unsteady, I get frustrated because it so often challenges my faith. And right now, my confidence is waning because this has been a tough season. I feel unsettled about some important issues, and I want to face them with strength and courage. So please bolster my weakness with Your Word. In Jesus' name. Amen.

No need to panic over alarms or surprises, or predictions that doomsday's just around the corner, because GOD will be right there with you; he'll keep you safe and sound.
PROVERBS 3:25-26 MSG

TODAY'S FOCUS POINT

My confidence is in God.

Sweet Friendship

Father God, I want to be a good friend. Not only is that my heart's desire, but I also want good friends for me too. Friendship just makes life sweeter in every way. So open my eyes to see Your provision for this and open my heart to embrace those You bring into my community. You know the struggles I've had with friends in the past, so I'm trusting for the right women. Not that I'm looking for perfection. But I do want friends who value purposeful relationships.

Let me surround myself with women who seek to love rather than hold on to offenses. My hope is for a group who always believes the best of one another. Create for me a group who chooses to rally together in support during the challenging seasons. Bring me a group of women seeking intimacy, desiring to have a deeper heart connection. And let nothing divide us, be it gossip or any other kind of betrayal. In Jesus' name. Amen.

He who covers and forgives an offense seeks love, but he who repeats or gossips about a matter separates intimate friends.
PROVERBS 17:9 AMP

TODAY'S FOCUS POINT

Be the kind of friend I want.

The Perfect Motivation

Father God, bless me with heavenly perspective today. Help me see the value in what needs to be done, and bless me with the motivation to do it. Sometimes I lose inspiration because the task ahead is uninteresting and I'm bored. Sometimes I lack the drive because I'm feeling overwhelmed with life and unable to find the gumption to get moving. And I don't always see the purpose for pushing through.

So thank You for today's passage of scripture. It helps me refocus to see a new way of approaching those unexciting tasks on my to-do list. Would You change my heart so my desire is to please You with each of those tasks? And help me recognize the blessings that will come from a good attitude in every assignment. Let it start today. In Jesus' name. Amen.

Whatever you do [whatever your task may be], work from the soul [that is, put in your very best effort], as [something done] for the Lord and not for men, knowing [with all certainty] that it is from the Lord [not from men] that you will receive the inheritance which is your [greatest] reward.
Colossians 3:23–24 AMP

TODAY'S FOCUS POINT

I'm doing this for the Lord.

A Servant's Heart

Father God, I confess my prideful attitude lately. Forgive me for thinking of myself as superhuman and self-important all while ignoring the truth that I am flawed in every way. That's not me being self-deprecating. I know You created me, and You don't make junk. But I have thought too much of myself for too long, and I'm ready to surrender to Your will for my life. I'm ready to get serious about my faith and let You lead me.

Today, will You renew my heart? Will You bathe me in humility? Teach me to adopt a servant's attitude in how I live and love, so I won't see myself as more important than anyone else. I get down on my knees today, asking You to be my shepherd—my north star. God, the fun and games are over, and my heart is submitted to Your leadership. Mature my faith to bless me and glorify You. I am Yours. In Jesus' name. Amen.

Hit bottom, and cry your eyes out. The fun and games are over. Get serious, really serious. Get down on your knees before the Master; it's the only way you'll get on your feet.
JAMES 4:9–10 MSG

TODAY'S FOCUS POINT

How can I serve others today?

Delivered from Despair

Father God, thank You for being such a compassionate Father, meeting me in my deep despair. Thank You that when I cry out in pain or heartache You always hear me, even from the heavens. I'm so grateful I serve a God who deeply cares when my world feels too big. Thank You for rescuing me when I'm overwhelmed and hopeless.

When I think back over my life, I see all the times You showed up for me in meaningful ways. I remember the moments when You swooped in at the last minute to save the day. Even when I cried crocodile tears about things that now seem insignificant, You treated me with care. You've always showed such deep compassion, no matter what I was dealing with. And today, as I look back, my heart is overflowing with thanksgiving. Every time I needed help, You showed me You're God in the big and small moments of despair. You never once ignored me. In Jesus' name. Amen.

In my distress I cried out to you, the delivering God,
and from your temple-throne you heard my troubled
cry, and my sobs went right into your heart.
PSALM 18:6 TPT

TODAY'S FOCUS POINT

My sobs penetrate God's heart.

The Greatest Joy

Father God, scripture tells me to find joy in the difficulties I face, but that seems counterintuitive. It says hardship is an invaluable opportunity to experience extreme joy, but how can that be? Would You talk to me today about this? Would You speak into my heart about how I can find gladness in the middle of my mess?

I'd love to sense my heart being settled even when the world around me feels chaotic. I would love to rise above what is weighing me down. And I know that because You say it can be, as a believer I'm capable of having the greatest joy even in the toughest times. It's not that I'm excited things are rough. Instead, it's that I'm joyous because I trust You are intervening on my behalf. I'm not alone in the trials. You're with me at all times. And that is the source of the joy that pours out of my heart. In Jesus' name. Amen.

My fellow believers, when it seems as though you are facing nothing but difficulties, see it as an invaluable opportunity to experience the greatest joy that you can!
JAMES 1:2 TPT

TODAY'S FOCUS POINT

I can have joy in the grueling.

Social Media Insecurity

Father God, this struggle with insecurity has lasted a long time. It's nothing new. And I recognize that what drives it is that I constantly compare myself to others, and it consumes me. Social media has done me no favors in this department because it's in my face every time I pick up my phone.

Even knowing people share their best moments online, I often compare them to my worst moments in real life. Their kids are always succeeding. Their marriages look divine. Their landscaping and home decor are so inviting. And their lives look fun and full. Today, help me disconnect my value from the images others post on social media. Let my value rest in You alone. Help me see myself from Your perspective. In Jesus' name. Amen.

And here's why: you are still living in the flesh, not in the Spirit. How do I know? Are you fighting with one another? Are you comparing yourselves to others and becoming consumed with jealousy? Then it sounds like you are living in the flesh, no different from the rest who live by the standards of this rebellious and broken world.

1 Corinthians 3:3 voice

TODAY'S FOCUS POINT

Don't compare my worst to their best.

Why We Forgive Others

Father God, thank You for Jesus Christ and what His death on the cross did for me. That selfless act changed my life forever by offering me once-and-done forgiveness for my sins—past, present, and future. I recognize the weight of that pure gift! Nothing else can ever compare!

Knowing what You've done, I ask You to cultivate in me a willingness to extend grace to others. Jesus rescued and restored me through His love, so let me be generous to forgive when I've been wronged. Today, help me release all offenses in gratitude for what Your Son's blood did for me. Give me a heart for restoration. In Jesus' name. Amen.

Since we've compiled this long and sorry record as sinners (both us and them) and proved that we are utterly incapable of living the glorious lives God wills for us, God did it for us. Out of sheer generosity he put us in right standing with himself. A pure gift. He got us out of the mess we're in and restored us to where he always wanted us to be. And he did it by means of Jesus Christ.
ROMANS 3:23–24 MSG

TODAY'S FOCUS POINT

He forgave me, so I can forgive others.

God Will Guide Each Step

Father God, today I am choosing not to live in fear, for You are with me always. I don't have to know all the answers because You're my guiding light. I don't have to figure it all out because You already have. Why should I ever fear, when You clearly promise to navigate me through each step of my life with love and compassion?

So open my eyes to see the path You've cleared for me to walk. Even when it takes me through dark valleys, let Your light shine the way. It's Your wise teaching that will be my compass. And my mind and heart will find peace in the nighttime hours, knowing You will meet me in the morning and direct my day. You are a good, good Father, and I appreciate that You don't let Your sheep wander aimlessly. In Jesus' name. Amen.

I will bless the Eternal, whose wise teaching orchestrates my days and centers my mind at night. He is ever present with me; at all times He goes before me. I will not live in fear or abandon my calling because He stands at my right hand.
PSALM 16:7–8 VOICE

TODAY'S FOCUS POINT

God is my shepherd, and I will follow.

My Strength in Weakness

Father God, thank You that I don't have to count on my own strength to get me through the day. Because if that were the case, I'd be in big trouble. I recognize the limitations in place because of my humanity, and I see them as beneficial! Without my weakness, there would be nothing to drive me into Your arms for help. So I'm grateful You're always the bedrock beneath my feet.

Especially today, let me feel Your presence as my wonderful deliverer. There are some tough conversations coming up and I'm counting on You to be my rock of rescue where none can harm me. Be the shield around me. Be the mighty power that saves me. Give me the strength to use my words wisely and with confidence. For You are my faith-fortress, a safe place as I walk through difficulties in life. Thank You! In Jesus' name. Amen.

Yahweh, you're the bedrock beneath my feet, my faith-fortress, my wonderful deliverer, my God, my rock of rescue where none can reach me. You're the shield around me, the mighty power that saves me, and my high place.
PSALM 18:2 TPT

TODAY'S FOCUS POINT

My strength comes from God.

When Anger Interferes with Life

Father God, in those moments when anger threatens to control my emotions, please stop it. Give me clarity to see what's happening so I'm able to slow my response to a situation. Help me take a step back and a deep breath for perspective. I don't want the enemy to control me through my temper because that's destructive on every level.

Even more, teach me to release offenses rather than keep score of all the ways I've been wronged. Life is hard enough without filling my time with vengeful thoughts. And keeping track of everyone's shortcomings does nothing to create a caring community. Relationships are precious and important, and I don't want my anger to cause a rift that may be irreparable. Nor do I want the enemy to succeed in manipulating me to be passionate about the wrong things. In Jesus' name. Amen.

But don't let the passion of your emotions lead you to sin! Don't let anger control you or be fuel for revenge, not for even a day. Don't give the slanderous accuser, the Devil, an opportunity to manipulate you!
EPHESIANS 4:26–27 TPT

TODAY'S FOCUS POINT

Anger will not control me.

Discerning Right from Wrong

Father God, in today's world it's getting harder and harder to discern right from wrong. The lines have been blurred, making it challenging to get a clear picture at times. I've become desensitized about some things, making me less able to recognize hard lines in the sand. This is why I'm asking for a greater measure of Your divine discernment. I need You to remind me which way to go.

As I go about my day, help me know the difference between good and evil. There are people who look to me for answers. They watch how I live and often follow suit. And the last thing I want to do is let You down and lead them on the wrong path. I pray my life choices—although terribly flawed at times—become a beacon of hope that points to You. For that, I must have keen discernment and wisdom. Give me ears to hear and eyes to see as I purpose to live righteously. In Jesus' name. Amen.

"Please give your servant a discerning mind in order to govern your people and to distinguish good from evil, because no one is able to govern this important people of yours without your help."
1 KINGS 3:9 CEB

TODAY'S FOCUS POINT

God's discernment is available to me.

The Trap of Comparison

Father God, deliver me from the trap of comparison. It's something that trips me up on the regular, and I'm tired of feeling lousy about myself. Why can't I just be comfortable in my own skin? While I'm so quick to let others off the hook, for some reason the standards I set for myself are too high. They're unattainable. And when I check myself against others, somehow I always fall short.

I want to see my true worth today. I want to understand the value that I hold in Your eyes. Rather than beat myself up for being human, let me learn to love who You created me to be—stumbles, fumbles, and all. And let me appreciate that I am made different by design. It's not a weakness and design flaw. It's a uniqueness You decided for me. That makes me incomparable! In Jesus' name. Amen.

For we would never dare to compare ourselves with people who have based their worth on self-commendation. They check themselves against and compare themselves with one another. It just shows that they don't have any sense!
2 Corinthians 10:12 voice

TODAY'S FOCUS POINT

God made me different on purpose.

Walking with Humility

Father God, humility is often challenging. It's not that I always want a pat on the back, but I do appreciate someone noticing a job well done. I do like it when others notice the changes I've made. And it encourages me when I'm seen and known, recognized for the part I played in the situation. Is that wrong?

Maybe what You're asking is that I give credit where it's due. You're the one who blessed me with the talents I possess. You put me on the kingdom calendar at this moment in time for a reason. You blessed me with a desire to do good work and serve others. You are who directed my steps that opened the doors of opportunity. So since those are all true, let me walk with humility because I know You are my source of everything I must give to others. In Jesus' name. Amen.

No. He has told you, mortals, what is good in
His sight. What else does the Eternal ask of you
but to live justly and to love kindness and to
walk with your True God in all humility?
MICAH 6:8 VOICE

TODAY'S FOCUS POINT

God is my source and enabler!

When I Struggle to Feel Worthy

Father God, today's verse challenges me to change my perspective on who I am. And honestly, it's not an easy shift to make! I was raised hearing about my flaws and failures as a child, which followed me into adulthood. For so long, I've focused on the places I fall short, and I don't know how to let those go. But You do.

Lord, please speak into those deep places of pain and tell me I am good. Help me replace worldly lies with Your truth every day. Keep my eyes focused on who You say I am and not the hurtful things others say about me. And give me the grace to accept my imperfections and expect nothing less. The goal of life isn't to be perfect. Instead, it's to be full of purpose and passion for You! And with Your help, I'll have confidence unmatched by any short-lived solution the world offers. In Jesus' name. Amen.

I thank you, God, for making me so mysteriously complex! Everything you do is marvelously breathtaking. It simply amazes me to think about it! How thoroughly you know me, Lord!
Psalm 139:14 TPT

TODAY'S FOCUS POINT

I am imperfectly perfect.

Asking for God's Favor

Father God, bless me with the favor You gave to Moses. Would You give me favor with those in authority over me? Would You give me the same with my peers and those who look up to me for instruction and support? Allow them to see Your favor on me in meaningful ways and honor it as if they are honoring You directly.

Let me feel the anointing as I go about the business of my day. Please cover me with Your favor as I open my mouth to speak, and let it also be what gives me ears to hear the hearts of others. Let it influence my decisions so they continually bring You glory. And let it empower me to follow You faithfully no matter what comes my way. I seek Your love and favor above all else today. My hope is to steward it well as I shine a light on Your holy name with intentionality. In Jesus' name. Amen.

The LORD said to Moses, "I'll do exactly what you've asked because you have my special approval, and I know you by name."
EXODUS 33:17 CEB

TODAY'S FOCUS POINT

God's favor rests on me today!

Living by Faith

Father God, help me live by faith rather than by placing my trust in what I can see. For too long, I've relied on people to save me. I've looked to them for wisdom and insight. I have taken their advice to heart without listening to You for confirmation. Even with their heart in the right place, I realize they aren't my savior. I have expected governments to have solutions for better living. I've counted on laws and rules. My hope has been in organizations or churches.

Today I confess I've relied too much on my eyesight rather than my faith. From the condition of my relationships to the state of my health to my financial struggles, don't let me rely on what I see. Instead, Lord, help me reset my priorities in ways that nurture my belief in Your sovereignty. Let them reflect Your goodness. Let the ways I live and the things I say reveal my love for You. In Jesus' name. Amen.

That's why we're always full of courage. Even while we're at home in the body, we're homesick to be with the Master—for we live by faith, not by what we see with our eyes.
2 CORINTHIANS 5:6–7 TPT

TODAY'S FOCUS POINT

Trust the Lord over everything.

His Protection from Harm

Father God, please be my protection. I feel exposed and unsafe because of the stressful situations I'm trying to navigate right now. My heart is anxious thinking about the horrible outcomes and endings that may be on the horizon. I'm worried my key relationships may suffer because these circumstances are taxing. I'm concerned for my emotional and mental health. What I need, God, is to know I am secure under Your watchful eye.

Scripture says You will hide me within the shelter of Your embrace. Your arms will engulf me and surround me in Your care. And that's right where I want to be today. I'm seeking Your help for a peaceful heart. I'm craving a safe space where I can rest in Your presence. Fear has no dominion over my life any longer, because my kind and generous Father has filled every nook and cranny with His love. In Jesus' name. Amen.

Protect me from harm; keep an eye on me as you would a child who is reflected in the twinkling of your eye. Yes, hide me within the shelter of your embrace, under your outstretched wings.
PSALM 17:8 TPT

TODAY'S FOCUS POINT

God is my shelter.

In the Waiting

Father God, scripture tells me not to be impatient, but that's a very tall order. There's often a sense of urgency that drives me to want an immediate response. The truth is that I'm eager for closure. I'm desperate for there to be a resolution. And sometimes it's frustrating as I wait for You because our timing never seems to jibe. Waiting is hard, even though I know Your timing is always perfect. What's more, experience reminds me there are invaluable lessons to learn along the way. Any rush decision from You would negate those golden nuggets.

So today, help me endure. Align my heart with Yours. Bless me with stamina as I wait for Your holy hand to move on my behalf. And help me not lose hope because it's taking longer than I would like. You're not a God who disappoints! I will wait and trust You all the more. In Jesus' name. Amen.

Here's what I've learned through it all: Don't give up; don't be impatient; be entwined as one with the Lord. Be brave and courageous, and never lose hope. Yes, keep on waiting—for he will never disappoint you!
PSALM 27:14 TPT

TODAY'S FOCUS POINT

Look for lessons in the waiting.

Thank God for Courage

Father God, because of You I'm not afraid of what may be coming around the corner. I've learned through Your Word, time in prayer, and past experiences that You've got me no matter what. I am safe and cared for. And this amazing promise lets me rest in Your arms even when chaos surrounds me. I have courage because You have created it in me. God, You are why my heart is steadfast and assured in tumultuous times.

Thank You for inviting me into the adventure of faith. It's been a beautiful and challenging journey that has grown me as a believer. It's taught me to be brave. And I appreciate how You instilled courage in me, teaching me to stand strong in Your strength. God, You used the ups and downs along the way to mature my confidence into a formidable force, and I'm better for it. So please continue to make me bold so I'm able to weather any storm. In Jesus' name. Amen.

He will not fear bad news; his heart is steadfast, trusting [confidently relying on and believing] in the LORD.
PSALM 112:7 AMP

TODAY'S FOCUS POINT

Trust over fear, every time.

Always Joy

Father God, thank You for my good life! It sure hasn't been easy, but it's been wonderful all the same. And that's completely because of You and the promise of joy even in the middle of trials. I may never be excited about going through them, but I'm thankful for Your guiding light. I may never hope for more hardships, but in them I will rejoice over the ways You steady and comfort me. There's nothing fun about heartache, but You bring gladness to my soul that calms my anxiousness.

Today You are enough. In fact, You're all I need. And whether in the dark valley or on the mountaintop, I can be at rest in Your arms. When I choose to release control because I trust that You are working, I'm at peace. My circumstances don't change the fullness of my heart because Your presence never leaves me. And I will forever rejoice in that! In Jesus' name. Amen.

This is a good life—my heart is glad, my soul is full of joy, and my body is at rest. Who could want for more?
PSALM 16:9 VOICE

TODAY'S FOCUS POINT

Life is good even when it's hard.

A Desire to Create Harmony

Father God, help me create harmony today. Let every interaction—even the ones that are often frustrating and tense—end on a good note. My desire is to show the compassion of Jesus to everyone. I crave to have one accord with those I love the most. Give me a sympathetic spirit so I'm able to bring care and concern into my conversations.

This world is harsh, and kindness is hard to come by. So let me be Your instrument, loving other believers and encouraging them in their battles. Let me be Your hands and feet, promoting Your goodness in the world. I don't want this for any fame. I'm not looking for praise. My heart is for others who need to know they are seen by You and deeply loved. Open my eyes so I'm able to see opportunities to bless those around me, helping to create harmony in their hearts. In Jesus' name. Amen.

Finally, all of you be of one mind, sympathetic, lovers of your fellow believers, compassionate, and modest in your opinion of yourselves.
1 PETER 3:8 CEB

TODAY'S FOCUS POINT

How can I create harmony?

Saying Goodbye to Guilt

Father God, I've had a long-standing relationship with guilt. It's been a constant companion as far back as I can remember. And You've watched as it often pulled me underwater. Every mistake or miscalculation became a reason to beat myself up incessantly. Even though I knew I was imperfect and forgiven, I couldn't release those guilty feelings.

Thank You for the powerful and timely reminder found in today's verse. The voice of condemnation no longer has a hold on me because I am Yours. As a believer, I have received freedom from feelings of guilt because of Jesus' finished work on the cross. And the truth is that Your expectations are for me to live a life of passion and purpose. . .not a life of perfection. Today moving forward, help me close my ears to the enemy's voice blaming me at every turn. He's no longer going to control how I feel. Help me stand in liberty and turn my ears and eyes to You. In Jesus' name. Amen.

So now the case is closed. There remains no accusing voice of condemnation against those who are joined in life-union with Jesus, the Anointed One.
ROMANS 8:1 TPT

TODAY'S FOCUS POINT

Guilt is not from God.

Not Sparking Jealousy

Father God, let every aspect of my life be an advertisement for You! The words I speak and the ways I act—may it all point to Your goodness and not mine. The only things I want to brag about are all the ways You're awesome. I want to boast about the times You showed up in my difficult circumstances. Any strength in me is from You. Any wisdom or discernment I display comes from seeking Your face. My ability to love and forgive is a gift from You alone. And my life transformed is the work of Your capable and loving hands.

Even more, let these truths be what keeps me humble so nothing on my part causes jealousy. Don't let me spark comparison in the heart of another. Instead, make Your blessings in my life evidence of Your generosity so the credit is never mine to take! In Jesus' name. Amen.

If you consider yourself to be wise and one who understands the ways of God, advertise it with a beautiful, fruitful life guided by wisdom's gentleness. Never brag or boast about what you've done and you'll prove that you're truly wise.

JAMES 3:13 TPT

TODAY'S FOCUS POINT

Give God all the credit.

Wanting God's Approval

Father God, help me remember that You are the only one I need to please. My desire for approval should rest with You alone. I confess the years I've spent trying to catch the eye of others. I've tried hard to impress the wrong people. And at times, I've compromised what I knew was right to do so. Help me set my priorities in the right order so I stay true to my faith and calling. Keep my eyes on You; keep me wanting to do what is right.

Today I need to know You approve of me. Despite all my imperfections, speak into my heart with kind words of affirmation so I feel Your love. Remind me that I am accepted and that my pursuit of righteous living pleases You. And let Your approval empower me to live in ways that glorify Your name and spread the good news. In Jesus' name. Amen.

Rather, we have been examined and approved by God to be trusted with the good news, and that's exactly how we speak. We aren't trying to please people, but we are trying to please God, who continues to examine our hearts.
1 Thessalonians 2:4 CEB

TODAY'S FOCUS POINT

Pleasing God informs how I live.

Living in His Favor

Father God, be my strength every morning as my eyes open to a new day. Let me wake with an unmistakable understanding that Your favor rests on me. Even if yesterday was hard and my night's sleep was terrible, assure me that You are well pleased with me. Even when I mess up horribly and end up causing trouble, let me wake knowing I am deeply loved by You no matter what. And in those times when I feel stuck in a season of sinning, let the Holy Spirit's conviction come with a dose of Your compassion.

More than anything else, I want to feel Your presence in my life. Guide me. Direct me. Save me. Restore me. Grow my faith. And strengthen me through the ups and downs in life, filling me with hope for something better. As long as You are with me, I will be okay. My heart is Yours because Your favor is mine. I love You so much, Father. In Jesus' name. Amen.

LORD, show us favor; we hope in you. Be our strength every morning, our salvation in times of distress.
ISAIAH 33:2 CEB

TODAY'S FOCUS POINT

Ask for God's favor in everything.

Humility Is Precious to God

Father God, I realize how precious humility is to You. I see how honoring it is because it recognizes Your position as Father and my position as child. It's void of haughtiness. It comes from a place of surrender rather than pride. And it shows respect for the mighty and wondrous ways about You. Let me always approach Your throne with a meek spirit, giving You the glory for everything good in my life.

Today I'm humbly seeking Your help to live righteously. I'm embarrassed that I still struggle with some of the same things. But I know Your promise is to help and heal, and that's what I'm asking. Let my life pay tribute to You in every way. From my words to my actions to my thought life, help me turn from my wicked ways and be healed. Help me be free from the struggles that keep me in bondage to sin. In Jesus' name. Amen.

If my people who belong to me will humbly pray, seek my face, and turn from their wicked ways, then I will hear from heaven, forgive their sin, and heal their land.
2 Chronicles 7:14 ceb

TODAY'S FOCUS POINT

Show humility when approaching God.

When You Need Motivation

Father God, this phrase is always on my mind right now: *I just don't wanna do it*. And honestly, that's exactly how I feel in this season. I don't want to keep trying in relationships that are frustrating. I don't have the desire to work harder when I keep getting passed over for the promotion. I don't have the patience or creativity to parent my kids who are difficult right now. I don't want to exercise or eat right. I don't want to grocery shop, prepare meals, or keep a clean house. I don't even want to socialize with my friends. I'm tired of adulting, and I want to hide away instead.

Unless You lovingly change my heart today and motivate me for action, I'm stuck. I don't want to be a quitter, but my get-up-and-go has got up and gone. Renew my energy, Father. Give me an excitement for my life. Restore my desire to live and love well. I'm desperate for Your motivation in this season. In Jesus' name. Amen.

Don't burn out; keep yourselves fueled and aflame.
Be alert servants of the Master, cheerfully expectant.
Don't quit in hard times; pray all the harder. Help
needy Christians; be inventive in hospitality.
ROMANS 12:11–13 MSG

TODAY'S FOCUS POINT

God will reenergize me.

Confident and Obedient Faith

Father God, give me the kind of faith that You would call strong, just like the woman in today's verse. She didn't have to see You in action. She didn't demand You work in a specific way. Instead, she laid her petition out for Your intervention and trusted. Even though her daughter's situation was dire and terrifying, she didn't allow panic to grab hold of her. She didn't get bossy or grapple for control. Rather than lose her ever-lovin' mind, she simply chose to trust Your will and ways. I want to be like that.

Give me an extra measure of faith so I'm able to weather any storm that comes my way. Settle my heart so it believes in Your goodness. Open my eyes to see Your miracles and wonders. And give me the confidence to believe You can and will bless my obedient faith. In Jesus' name. Amen.

Then Jesus answered her, "Dear woman, your faith is strong! What you desire will be done for you." And at that very moment, her daughter was instantly set free from demonic torment.
MATTHEW 15:28 TPT

TODAY'S FOCUS POINT

I know God can do anything He wants.

Courage When You Need It

Father God, I know You're the one who will fill me with courage at the right time. When I need You to, You'll make me bold in faith to tackle what needs to be tackled. I don't have to muster up courage on my own. It's not up to me to find a brave bone in my body. And no matter how much I try, without Your strength and power coursing through my veins I'll fail to be fearless in tough moments. The truth is that I need You to infuse me with the nerve. You will always be my source for good things.

So today, fill me with courage to face my day. Help me steward it well so it benefits me rather than me using it to bully others. This isn't a desire to strong-arm anyone to get my way. Instead, it's a desire for me to find my footing to stand up and advocate for myself and those I care about. And when opportunities present themselves, give me the right words to share the gospel with confidence. In Jesus' name. Amen.

They finished their prayer, and immediately the whole place where they had gathered began to shake. All the disciples were filled with the Holy Spirit, and they began speaking God's message with courageous confidence.
ACTS 4:31 VOICE

TODAY'S FOCUS POINT

My confidence comes directly from God.

The Blessing of Discernment

Father God, today, please bless me with the ability to discern right from wrong. Even when the line between them is blurred, allow me to see the path You've laid out clearly. Please share Your unmatched and unquestionable knowledge when I need it most. The truth is that I'm lost without Your guidance. Without access to Your wisdom, my choices will be a shot in the dark. And because I am trying to live a righteous life that glorifies You every day, I want my decisions to reflect thoughtful choices.

Starting today, I want to focus on doing things that really matter—the things with an earthly blessing and an eternal pay-off. Help me love others with purpose and passion. Help me be generous with my time and treasure. Help my life preach of my love for You. And help me live a sincere and blameless life that pleases You! In Jesus' name. Amen.

This is my prayer: that your love might become even more and more rich with knowledge and all kinds of insight. I pray this so that you will be able to decide what really matters and so you will be sincere and blameless on the day of Christ.
PHILIPPIANS 1:9–10 CEB

TODAY'S FOCUS POINT

I need God's discernment.

A Spirit of Forgiveness

Father God, today's verse convicted me! The Holy Spirit did His job by calling me out, and I didn't see it coming. And while it doesn't feel good right now, I'm thankful You love me enough to convict me.

I confess there have been many times throughout my life when I've gloated, happy to see someone I didn't like fall. I have rejoiced over their failings and shortcomings and then shared it with others gleefully. There may even have been a smirk on my face when the news of their demise came my way. Lord, I've even giggled when a rival was embarrassed; I delighted in their fiasco. And I am so sorry. I don't want to be this kind of woman. Please reveal any unforgiveness in my spirit so You can heal it. Let me release any offense so I can extend grace and a helping hand. I want to love like You do. In Jesus' name. Amen.

Never gloat when your enemy meets disaster,
and don't be quick to rejoice if he falls.
PROVERBS 24:17 TPT

TODAY'S FOCUS POINT

There's no celebration when someone falls.

Building an Obedient Life

Father God, help me be more obedient when I know You're trying to guide me. There have been times I felt You speaking right into my spirit, but I ignored it. I felt You leading me in a certain direction, but I overlooked it. And at times I even stood in agreement, excited to walk out Your plan, but then changed my mind. I got distracted with life or scared to step out of my comfort zone. Forgive me.

I know Your words are foundational. They are important. And they ground me, serving as anchors when life gets bumpy. When You speak, let it catch my attention. Let my focus immediately shift to You over everything else. And make Your words dear to my heart so I treasure each one with reverence. I want to get serious about building my life through obedience to You. Let me start today. In Jesus' name. Amen.

"Why are you so polite with me, always saying 'Yes, sir,'
and 'That's right, sir,' but never doing a thing I tell you?
These words I speak to you are not mere additions to your
life, homeowner improvements to your standard of living.
They are foundation words, words to build a life on."
LUKE 6:46–47 MSG

TODAY'S FOCUS POINT

I will listen to and obey God's words.

The Desire for Friendship

Father God, I love the picture of friendship painted in today's scripture. Having a solid community makes life so much better. When I'm struggling, they're the ones to support me. When I don't know how to move forward, they help me navigate the next steps. When my heart is broken, they help pick up the pieces. Friends weep together. They grieve together. And they care for one another when the storms hit hard.

I want that, Lord. Today, hear my cry for a blessed community of like-minded women to walk through life with. Open my eyes to see them and open my heart to receive them. In Jesus' name. Amen.

Two are better than one because they have a good return for their hard work. If either should fall, one can pick up the other. But how miserable are those who fall and don't have a companion to help them up! Also, if two lie down together, they can stay warm. But how can anyone stay warm alone? Also, one can be overpowered, but two together can put up resistance. A three-ply cord doesn't easily snap.
ECCLESIASTES 4:9-12 CEB

TODAY'S FOCUS POINT

Ask God to bring community.

Every Good Thing Comes from God

Father God, forgive me for not always giving You thanks. Too often, I just move on and forget to stop and acknowledge Your hand in a situation. Sometimes I give the credit to the wrong people or influences and have even taken the credit myself. And still there are times I don't recognize that I need to be grateful at all.

Help me remember that every good thing comes from You! Let me be quick to say thank You when a parenting situation ends well. Let me speak out appreciation when my path crosses with the right person at the right time. Allow me to have a grateful heart when there is resolution in a relationship, promotion in a job, and healing in a health situation. Even if I'm blessed by another, let me thank You for the behind-the-scenes work. You are good, all the time. In Jesus' name. Amen.

You are my God, and I give You thanks; You are my God, and I praise You. Give thanks to our Eternal Lord; He is always good. He never ceases to be loving and kind.
PSALM 118:28–29 VOICE

TODAY'S FOCUS POINT

Thank God for every good thing.

Comparing God's Created

Father God, it's exhausting to compare myself to others like I do. It's been part of my DNA for so long now that You're the only one who can change it. Being made in Your image is a beautiful blessing. Having Your likeness in my blueprint is a breathtaking truth. What a tragedy that I still consider myself less than others. If I see someone, I'll compare her wardrobe to mine. I may look at her body and decide I don't measure up to her fitness level. I compare my stuff to her stuff and see only what I lack. Her car is cooler. Her vacations are to better places. She hangs out with the in-crowd. . . . For some reason, I never come out on top.

Today, let me see the goodness You baked into me. I want to be happy with who You created me to be. I'm an original, not like anyone else. Help me see that as a good thing! In Jesus' name. Amen.

*So God created man in His own image, in the
image and likeness of God He created him;
male and female He created them.*
GENESIS 1:27 AMPC

TODAY'S FOCUS POINT

By design, I'm like no other.

Thankful for Community!

Father God, thank You for the community You've placed in my life. I'm not sure I recognize them often enough, but I want to make this a regular part of prayer. It's Your loving kindness that has knit my heart together with theirs. It's Your provision that has made it possible to surround myself with such compassionate people. And I'm grateful You saw fit to bless me with these friends and family. Let me be a blessing back!

Help me place a high priority on loving them as best as I can. Allow me to defend and uphold them as well as cheer them on. Help me be generous, ready to support them however and whenever they need it. Let me be interested in their lives and always looking for opportunities to engage with them in meaningful ways. And let me humbly bring their requests to Your throne room, making sure to pray for them with fervor. I'm so grateful to have a loving group to surround me. In Jesus' name. Amen.

We always thank God for all of you when we mention you constantly in our prayers.
1 Thessalonians 1:2 CEB

TODAY'S FOCUS POINT

Pray for the people I love.

The Problem with Busyness

Father God, let my busy calendar be full of purpose and passion. An eventful life is a beautiful thing, but it can also be unwise at times! So guide me as I fill it with to-dos that have Your stamp of approval. Let me be prayerful as I begin to fill things in. My desire is that it benefits me and others as well as blesses You. Let each commitment I choose to walk out today bring You honor.

Would You give me wisdom and discernment as I create my schedule? Sometimes I get overly excited at the plans in place, only to end up exhausted because it's too much. That leads to me making up excuses to cancel obligations altogether or try and push to another time. Help me be careful to gauge my bandwidth so I make the most of the time I've been given. In Jesus' name. Amen.

Look carefully then how you walk! Live purposefully and worthily and accurately, not as the unwise and witless, but as wise (sensible, intelligent people), making the very most of the time [buying up each opportunity], because the days are evil.
EPHESIANS 5:15–16 AMPC

TODAY'S FOCUS POINT

Be wise as I fill my calendar.

When You Don't Like Who You Love

Father God, today's verse convicts me in the best of ways. Thank You for Your well-timed and perfectly placed messages. This is one I really needed to hear! So let the words of truth sink deep into my DNA so I can live this out in real time.

I'll be honest, right now it's hard for me to like certain people that I love. They are dismissive when I'm trying to connect. They don't want to invest time to grow our relationship. They're selfish and self-focused, completely unaware of my needs. But they are important to me, and I love them dearly. Help me endure this season with them. Give me hope that things can change. And let me trust that You will bring the necessary healing at the right time, restoring us and our relationship. My vow is to love no matter what. Even when it feels fruitless, as long as You tell me to do so, I will love without fail. In Jesus' name. Amen.

Love puts up with anything and everything that comes along; it trusts, hopes, and endures no matter what.
1 CORINTHIANS 13:7 VOICE

TODAY'S FOCUS POINT

Love no matter what.

The Trap of Fear

Father God, I'm tired of falling prey to fear. It's frustrating how easily it pops up, especially when I didn't see it coming. I know what Your Word says about activating faith over fear. I've read the powerful verses that tell me not to be afraid. I've talked with You at length about what pushes my worry button. I have friends and family who have prayed with me and over me. And here I stand today, still battling the same thing.

So I'm taking a new approach. Father, grow my confidence in You! Let me know without a doubt that You won't let me fall. I am placing my trust in Your abilities, believing You're in control. And while I may not know how You will save me, I know You will. I don't need the answers because they're all found in You. Fear and intimidation can no longer trap me because my trust is rooted in the goodness of my Father. In Jesus' name. Amen.

Fear and intimidation is a trap that holds you back. But when you place your confidence in the Lord, you will be seated in the high place.
PROVERBS 29:25 TPT

TODAY'S FOCUS POINT

Faith will always triumph over fear.

Glorious Grit

Father God, it's days like these when I'm so ready for Jesus to come back! I'm ready to just throw in the towel and be done. I want to hide under the covers and wave the white flag in defeat. But then I run into today's verses, and I'm reminded that a supernatural perseverance is available to every believer. When I ask, You will give me glorious grit to stick it out. So today, I'm asking.

Everything feels harder right now. The world seems crazier. The burdens seem weightier. And I'm feeling the pressure of it all pressing down on me. God, lift these off as I choose to focus on Your goodness. Life is challenging, but with You, there is a way to navigate life with a victory mindset. Show me that today. Give me determination to stand strong and not back down. Fill me with resolve. Bless me with endurance. In Jesus' name. Amen.

Though we experience every kind of pressure, we're not crushed. At times we don't know what to do, but quitting is not an option. We are persecuted by others, but God has not forsaken us. We may be knocked down, but not out.
2 Corinthians 4:8–9 TPT

TODAY'S FOCUS POINT

With God, I can endure anything.

Praying about Anxiety

Father God, my heart is heavy today. Instead of praying about everything, I'm worrying about everything. I've buried these struggles deep in my heart, when I should be sharing them with You every chance I get. I'm clinging to them with all my might, trying to fix them in my own strength. And God, they are too much for me to carry alone. I'm losing sleep, and I'm unable to focus on my daily tasks. Please hear my prayer today and let Your peace fall on me!

Give me the courage to release every anxious thought into Your capable hands. Give me confidence, knowing You are working on my behalf to straighten the crooked path. I can trust You with my fears and stressors because You are always for me. In Your loving-kindness, You're able to calm my anxious heart and strengthen my faith in significant ways. In Jesus' name. Amen.

Don't be anxious about things; instead, pray. Pray about everything. He longs to hear your requests, so talk to God about your needs and be thankful for what has come. And know that the peace of God (a peace that is beyond any and all of our human understanding) will stand watch over your hearts and minds in Jesus, the Anointed One.
PHILIPPIANS 4:6–7 VOICE

TODAY'S FOCUS POINT

Pray about every anxious thought.

God's Protection Won't Quit

Father God, You are a mighty warrior, always ready to defend those You love. You are a shepherd, protective of every sheep in the flock. You are a father, prepared to defend Your children at a moment's notice. And I am so thankful to be covered by Your unmatched love, compassion, and protection!

Thank You for being willing to get in the trenches with me. There are few who will, and I don't take it lightly. I'm learning there is no limit to what You'll do to shield me from harm. You keep me in Your sight, constantly monitoring my life and what comes into it. That's what a loving Father does for His kids, and it settles my heart to know You will finish what You've started in my life. Nothing can stop it! And nothing will make You quit caring for me. In Jesus' name. Amen.

When I walk into the thick of trouble, keep me alive in the angry turmoil. With one hand strike my foes, with your other hand save me. Finish what you started in me, GOD. Your love is eternal—don't quit on me now.
PSALM 138:7-8 MSG

TODAY'S FOCUS POINT

I am protected by God.

Bold, Courageous Faith

Father God, give me the courage to keep going. Life is so hard right now, and I'm tempted to give in and quit. I long for the easy button these days because it never is easy for me. It feels like I go from tragedy to frustration to heartbreak to worry. I can't seem to catch a break to get my breath. My heart is hurting, and my strength is failing.

Bolster me with Your love, Father! Reinforce my resolve. Help me walk the rocky paths of life with courageous faith, knowing You promise to reward those who do. I want to be a woman whose hope is in You. And I want my life to model that truth for others. So in those moments when I am fearful, fortify my confidence. When my battle with insecurity is overwhelming, bring blessed reassurance. Toughen me up so I'm able to thrive in my faith as I find my bravery in You. In Jesus' name. Amen.

So don't lose your bold, courageous faith, for you are destined for a great reward! You need the strength of endurance to reveal the poetry of God's will and then you receive the promise in full.
HEBREWS 10:35–36 TPT

TODAY'S FOCUS POINT

My courage in God brings rewards.

God Models Comfort

Father God, scripture says You are the God of all comfort. You're the one who meets us in our mess and calms our anxious hearts. You bring the spirit of peace into each chaotic situation, allowing us to find our footing again. And You teach us to comfort others because we were first comforted by You. God, every bit of compassion and care I'm able to share I learned from Your perfect parenting.

Today, open my eyes to see those who are struggling and weighed down by their circumstances. Give me the ability to show sympathy and not judgment. Through You, we are all here to support one another in sweet community. We are to be Your hands and feet to a needy world. So let me be quick to give a hug or hold a hand. Let my heart be made tender with compassion. In Jesus' name. Amen.

May the God and Father of our Lord Jesus Christ be blessed! He is the compassionate Father and God of all comfort. He's the one who comforts us in all our trouble so that we can comfort other people who are in every kind of trouble. We offer the same comfort that we ourselves received from God.
2 Corinthians 1:3–4 ceb

TODAY'S FOCUS POINT

I am equipped to comfort others.

Created on Purpose

Father God, when I start feeling like I'm not good enough when compared with others, remind me that I'm the product of Your hand. Because You created me with great intention, I can be confident in who I am. My insecurities don't have to get the best of me because I realize I'm here on purpose and for a purpose.

So when my heart begins to betray, causing me to question my worth, let me be quick to remember that my life was planned out. I'm not a mistake or an inconvenience. What's more, You have already made good blueprints for my future. I'm important enough to have been given tasks here on earth that are designed to glorify You in heaven. You've entrusted me with accomplishing divine doings in Your name. Thank You for reminding me that I have unmatched value. Today, I'm going to let that beautiful truth sink deep into my heart. And I'm going to stand tall because my identity is anchored in being Your beloved creation. In Jesus' name. Amen.

For we are the product of His hand, heaven's poetry etched on lives, created in the Anointed, Jesus, to accomplish the good works God arranged long ago.
EPHESIANS 2:10 VOICE

TODAY'S FOCUS POINT

God doesn't create junk.

Content with God

Father God, money is a big deal for so many people. While I struggle with wanting more at times, I'm actually content in what You've chosen to give me. It's not too much that I make idols out of stuff or try to keep up with others. Nor is it too little that I'm overwhelmed and stressed all the time. Somehow, my heart is content, and I feel blessed.

Today, I'm thankful that I'm not battling between serving You and serving money. I don't want anything to get between us because there's no earthly thing that could ever replace Your goodness in my life. So God, let my eyes always be open and focused on serving You with my life. Let my mind think only on Your kindness and generosity. And let my allegiance to You never be in question. You are the one who makes me happy and secure. In Jesus' name. Amen.

No one can serve two masters. If you try, you will wind up loving the first master and hating the second, or vice versa. People try to serve both God and money—but you can't. You must choose one or the other.
MATTHEW 6:24 VOICE

TODAY'S FOCUS POINT

All I want is more of God.

Choosing to Release Anxiety

Father God, thank You for today's verse that so powerfully reminds me that worry adds no value to my life. Anxiety has no positive result in my heart. I realize it doesn't make me feel better. It doesn't solve my problems. It doesn't make the issues disappear. Instead, it robs me of what I really need to feel better, which is a peaceful heart, a spirit of trust, and an unshakable faith.

Help me break the habit of falling into a state of worry at the drop of a hat. It's so frustrating that worry is always my default button. Next time, let my knees hit the floor the minute anxious thoughts begin to creep in. Keep me from entertaining them on any level because it's a trap that keeps me tangled and upset. It leaves me thinking up terrible outcomes. So starting today, my plan is to release worry into Your capable hands. That's exactly where it needs to be. In Jesus' name. Amen.

Worrying does not do any good; who here can claim to add even an hour to his life by worrying?
MATTHEW 6:27 VOICE

TODAY'S FOCUS POINT

Worrying adds no value to the situation.

God's Peace over the World's Anxiety

Father God, in today's world, how am I supposed to not let my heart be troubled? I feel like that goal sets me up for failure. It feels unattainable. And I'm afraid to set my sights on making it my goal because I fall short time and time again. But in faith, I'm asking You to help me find a way. I need to conquer this anxiousness that keeps me stuck in a loop of stress.

So today, Lord, I'm asking You for peace. I don't want the kind the world offers, for it is short lived and ineffective. I'm looking for Your peace that promises to calm my heart in significant ways. I don't want to be agitated by anxiety. I don't want to be disturbed by disquietness. I don't want to be unsettled by uneasiness. Instead, I am choosing to press into You for reassurance. You've got me, and I know it. In Jesus' name. Amen.

*Peace I leave with you; My [own] peace I now give
and bequeath to you. Not as the world gives do I give
to you. Do not let your hearts be troubled, neither let
them be afraid. [Stop allowing yourselves to be agitated
and disturbed; and do not permit yourselves to be
fearful and intimidated and cowardly and unsettled.]*
JOHN 14:27 AMPC

TODAY'S FOCUS POINT

Let peace reign in my heart.

Showing Off for Approval

Father God, stop me right in my tracks if I start to show off to get the approval of others. I don't want anyone's opinion to be so important that I must boast for recognition. I don't want to care if I'm noticed or not. So please humble me to live in authentic ways that glorify Your name and not mine. I'm not interested in impressing anyone but You. And I only want to impress You with my obedience. I want to show my love for You by living right and loving others well.

God, let the accolades of the world grow dim until they mean nothing. Today, let every choice I make be filtered through faith and not pride. I know a humble heart is of high value in Your economy, so let it also be in mine. Shut my mouth if I begin to brag for attention. And remove anything that makes me chase after the esteem of another. In Jesus' name. Amen.

Examine your motives to make sure you're not showing off when you do your good deeds, only to be admired by others; otherwise, you will lose the reward of your heavenly Father.
MATTHEW 6:1 TPT

TODAY'S FOCUS POINT

Seek the approval of God alone.

The Command of Courage

Father God, it's interesting that You command courage rather than merely suggest it. You don't just hope I find strength in trials; You order it. And because of Your great love demonstrated over time, this mandate doesn't feel mean spirited. It doesn't sound harsh or hateful. Instead, I hear it in different tones based on where I am in the moment. Sometimes it comes across gently, like You know what's best for me and are imploring that response. Other times it's a battle cry that challenges me to get up and be brave. Both are commands. But they hit me differently.

I love that what remains the same in every scenario is the reality of Your presence. It's the reason I can be courageous and strong no matter what. So today, let me remember You're with me every step of the way. Because of Your presence, nothing can terrorize me. I'm brave and strong through You. In Jesus' name. Amen.

"I've commanded you to be brave and strong,
haven't I? Don't be alarmed or terrified, because the
LORD your God is with you wherever you go."
JOSHUA 1:9 CEB

TODAY'S FOCUS POINT

God is with me all the time.

The Fountain of Hope

Father God, scripture says You are the fountain of hope that never runs dry. While I often think it's up to me to find ways to muster hope, the truth is that You're the one who fills me with it. And because of Your generosity, it will overflow. Joy and peace are part of the filling too, blessings that come from trusting You as my source. Then the Holy Spirit's continuous presence allows that hope to radiate within me. This is why I can live with confidence and courage.

As I wake today with a heaviness of spirit, hear me cry out to You for hope. I need it today, Lord. I need to know You're in control and things will get better. I need to know I'm held in Your mighty arms. Let me look to You for the hope, joy, and peace that's required to walk out my faith well. In Jesus' name. Amen.

Now may God, the fountain of hope, fill you to overflowing with uncontainable joy and perfect peace as you trust in him. And may the power of the Holy Spirit continually surround your life with his super-abundance until you radiate with hope!
ROMANS 15:13 TPT

TODAY'S FOCUS POINT

Hope comes from God alone.

Undistracted Devotion

Father God, this life is full of distractions. Every day, I'm faced with a million things that can derail me if I let them. And not all of them are bad! I have family obligations as well as household tasks. I have responsibilities at work and in the places I volunteer my time. And then I have personal items on my to-do list, like working out and doctor appointments. That's in addition to all the random things that pop up from day to day. Admittedly, sometimes You end up pushed to the bottom of the list.

But Lord, You deserve my undistracted devotion! So let this morning be the start of a shift in how I prioritize. I'm going to start the day with You, and it's going to set the tone moving forward. Open my eyes for ways to serve You. Open my ears to hear Your still, small voice. Let my love and dedication be undivided. In Jesus' name. Amen.

I am trying to help you and make things easier for you and not make things difficult, but so that you would have undistracted devotion, serving the Lord constantly with an undivided heart.
1 Corinthians 7:35 TPT

TODAY'S FOCUS POINT

Make God my number one priority.

Why I Can Trust God

Father God, there are so many things that scare me. I'm worried about some struggles that are appearing in key relationships. I'm scared about my financial situation. I'm afraid of change, and there's a lot of it in my life right now. I'm worried what others will think if they really know me. I am anxious about some health issues. And I feel like the world is heading in the wrong direction. What am I supposed to do?

The Word tells me to trust You. It encourages me to cling to You above everything else in those fearful and confusing moments. When I do, the fear that taunts me will dissipate as Your presence calms my anxious heart. Even more, it brings a unique perspective. It makes me realize there is no fear on earth that can override Your perfect protection. That means I can trust You in all things and at all times! In Jesus' name. Amen.

Whenever I'm afraid, I put my trust in you—in God, whose word I praise. I trust in God; I won't be afraid. What can mere flesh do to me?
PSALM 56:3-4 CEB

TODAY'S FOCUS POINT

When I trust God, there is peace.

Choosing Obedience

Father God, the Bible is clear that when we follow Your commands, it makes life better. Not necessarily easier, but better. It doesn't take away the hard seasons everyone has to walk through. But through our obedience, we are strengthened. As we submit to Your leadership, we will receive divinely inspired direction and wisdom.

Today, I'm listening for Your voice. I'm looking for Your leading. It hasn't always been this way, but my desire now is to abide by Your commands. I know they will guide me into a deeper relationship with You. I respect Your will and ways, Lord. And I'm ready to embrace the path You've determined for my life. I will trust You each step of the way. In Jesus' name. Amen.

"But this thing I did command them: 'Listen to and obey My voice, and I will be your God, and you shall be My people; and you will walk in all the way which I command you, so that it may be well with you.'"
JEREMIAH 7:23 AMP

TODAY'S FOCUS POINT

My obedience to God changes my life.

When I Can't Release Guilt

Father God, take this guilt from me. It's something I've struggled with as far back as I can remember. And it keeps me from experiencing all You have for me. Even though I know I am forgiven because of Jesus' sacrifice on the cross, guilt hangs over my head. The problem is I can't seem to forgive myself.

Help me embrace redemption. Help me better understand how the gift of salvation blesses me. I don't want just head knowledge, Lord. I want heart knowledge so I can experience true happiness and joy. If You no longer consider me guilty, then why do I? Show me how to release myself from guilt so I can live in the freedom Jesus brought. Show me how to stand in truth and grace. And show me how to love who You made me to be, even though I'm imperfect. In Jesus' name. Amen.

The one whose wrongdoing is forgiven, whose sin is covered over, is truly happy! The one the LORD doesn't consider guilty—in whose spirit there is no dishonesty—that one is truly happy!
PSALM 32:1-2 CEB

TODAY'S FOCUS POINT

As a believer, my guilt is gone.

Despair Won't Last Forever

Father God, Your Word tells me that despair won't last forever. Grief and sorrow are part of the human experience, but they won't follow me into eternity. I may face anguish in spades here, but it stays here. And thank You that while experiencing these hard seasons on earth, I can still find hope in You. You'll comfort me through them as You wipe every tear that falls.

Let me meditate on this good news today. Let this encourage my heart to stay strong and praise You for what You're doing in each hardship right now. As I cling to You, make me courageous and confident and full of peace. This tough time won't mark the rest of my life because You promise the old will pass away. I look forward to a renewal through You, and I stand ready to embrace it! In Jesus' name. Amen.

God will wipe away every tear from their eyes; and death shall be no more, neither shall there be anguish (sorrow and mourning) nor grief nor pain any more, for the old conditions and the former order of things have passed away.
REVELATION 21:4 AMPC

TODAY'S FOCUS POINT

There is hope for the future.

The Promise of Provision

Father God, help me relax as I find hope in Your promise to take care of me. Grow my confidence in Your goodness, which meets every need in the right ways and at the right time. I get so stressed, scared about how these tough circumstances will work themselves out. The truth is that I'm a doer, so waiting on You to move is hard for me. I'm used to providing for myself and finding ways to meet my own needs. Help me flex my faith muscle and trust You instead.

I've seen Your generosity. I've experienced Your kindness. I know You're able to bless me in remarkable ways. So today, let me step off the performance treadmill and trust in the fulfillment of Your promises. It's not that I can't take the right steps forward in obedience. But it's choosing to have a faithful heart as I do. In Jesus' name. Amen.

You can be sure that God will take care of everything you need, his generosity exceeding even yours in the glory that pours from Jesus. Our God and Father abounds in glory that just pours out into eternity. Yes.
PHILIPPIANS 4:19–20 MSG

TODAY'S FOCUS POINT

God will meet every need.

God's Strength in My Weakness

Father God, what a blessing to know my weakness isn't seen as a negative in Your eyes. In fact, You made me to be weak without You on purpose. I was created with serious human limitations. I'm supposed to need Your help to weather the storms of life. And while I am a strong woman, my strength is short lived and inadequate for this life. And I'm so grateful it is.

Today, strengthen me for what's ahead. Reinforce my resolve to meet challenges head-on. Fortify my faltering faith. Make me brave as I navigate the choppy waters. Give me courage to have the hard conversations and make the difficult decisions. And every step of the way, let me give You the glory for empowering me through the storms. I will boast of Your provision and brag about Your grace. For it has changed my life! In Jesus' name. Amen.

He said to me, "My grace is enough for you, because power is made perfect in weakness." So I'll gladly spend my time bragging about my weaknesses so that Christ's power can rest on me.
2 Corinthians 12:9 ceb

TODAY'S FOCUS POINT

I don't have to be strong on my own.

Seeking Strategic Friendships

Father God, help me choose my friends wisely. Help me walk with integrity the fine line of being discerning without being judgmental. I don't want to be snobby, but I do want to be selective. I understand the importance of surrounding myself with those who will encourage, rather than undermine, my relationship with You. The truth is we are who we hang out with. And I don't want anything or anyone to derail my pursuit of righteous living.

In the same vein, make me a good friend too! I want to add to the lives of others rather than take anything away. I want to be a positive influence. I want to be a source of truth and encouragement. I want to love others well. My desire is to link arms as we walk through the valleys and mountaintops together. Community is so important! So today, let's start the journey of finding the right friendships that will be a blessing for all involved. In Jesus' name. Amen.

So stop fooling yourselves! Evil companions
will corrupt good morals and character.
1 CORINTHIANS 15:33 TPT

TODAY'S FOCUS POINT

Be the kind of friend I want.

Fueled and Aflame to Persevere

Father God, good morning! Before I even put my feet on the floor, let me thank You for the gift of perseverance. Without it, I'd have given up awhile ago. . .like I usually do. I'm not built for waiting things out. I don't like to emotionally stay in one place for long, especially when it's unpleasant. And my past will show You that I've been quick to bail when times get tough. I just don't like those spaces. Rather than stick it out and trust You, I've walked away.

But today is different! I'm believing Your promise to strengthen me for every situation. I'm choosing to stand in victory. I'm awaiting the blessing that comes from steadfast endurance. And I'm ready to saturate myself in Your Word so I'm fueled and aflame to stand strong in demanding times. Even more, I'm excited to help others find the grit to persevere too. You are trustworthy and will come through. I know it. In Jesus' name. Amen.

Don't burn out; keep yourselves fueled and aflame.
Be alert servants of the Master, cheerfully expectant.
Don't quit in hard times; pray all the harder. Help
needy Christians; be inventive in hospitality.
Romans 12:11-13 msg

TODAY'S FOCUS POINT

I won't quit when it gets tough.

Maker and Maintainer of Peace

Father God, it's obvious that peace is a big deal to You. It's an important part of walking out our faith in ways that please You. And those who make peace and maintain peace are close to Your heart. So God, let me be a peacemaker.

I know that's a tall order in this world because it's so full of chaos and evil these days. It's challenging to create harmony when everyone is at odds. Finding common ground isn't easy. And having a spirit of reconciliation is often met with a hostile response. But with You, nothing is impossible. So bless me today with the grace to generate goodwill in the places You send me. Give me confidence to stand in gentle strength when my efforts aren't well received. And give me the perseverance to continue promoting peace wherever I go. I want to receive the blessing that comes from being a maker and maintainer of Your holy harmony. In Jesus' name. Amen.

Blessed (enjoying enviable happiness, spiritually prosperous—with life-joy and satisfaction in God's favor and salvation, regardless of their outward conditions) are the makers and maintainers of peace, for they shall be called the sons of God!
MATTHEW 5:9 AMPC

TODAY'S FOCUS POINT

Whenever possible, promote peace.

God above the Busy

Father God, above everything else, let me seek You. More than my tiring to-do list. More than the crazy calendar for my kids. More than the stressed schedule for my husband. More than the demanding datebook for my own work. More than the active agenda for everything else I'm juggling. More than any of these, let me seek You first and foremost.

While it's important for me to be present in the lives of my family and friends, I want to always recognize Your place above it all. God, You matter the most. I love them with all my heart, and my hope is for their happiness and success. But I want my heart to be hidden in You. You're my strong tower and hiding place. So today, let me be mindful to seek Your kingdom. Let my desire to seek Your righteousness be ever present. Because when I seek You first, everything else just falls into place. In Jesus' name. Amen.

"So above all, constantly seek God's kingdom and his righteousness, then all these less important things will be given to you abundantly."
MATTHEW 6:33 TPT

TODAY'S FOCUS POINT

Choose God first.

Don't Hit Back

Father God, help me be the kind of woman who discovers beauty in everyone. I don't think others are perfect, but I do know there is goodness in them. And while they may make me angry by their words or actions, it's usually not on purpose. I don't want to hit back when there's no real reason for it. Instead, I want to do my best to get along with everyone. Remind me that I'm not the judge, because I'm sinful too. I have no right to be in that position, especially knowing it's rightly Yours.

Today, fill me with peace so anger doesn't have any room to get a stronghold. Make me quick to extend grace rather than hold on to any offenses. And when hard conversations are called for, let me say my piece in truth and love and then move on. In Jesus' name. Amen.

Don't hit back; discover beauty in everyone.
If you've got it in you, get along with everybody.
Don't insist on getting even; that's not for you to do.
"I'll do the judging," says God. "I'll take care of it."
ROMANS 12:17-19 MSG

TODAY'S FOCUS POINT

Remember God is the judge.

Victory over Weakness

Father God, I love that You get it. It blesses me to know that when I pray to You about where I'm struggling, You have first-hand knowledge of it. You're able to connect with me on deeper levels. You have sympathy because You've experienced it—all of it. You've been tested in every way. And that means there is nothing I will face that You haven't faced first.

Let me stand in Your strength, claiming victory over every weakness I battle with today. Let me stand in solidarity with You. Let me cling to You for hope when it seems like nothing will ever change. And when I begin to feel overwhelmed and desperate, remind me that I can approach You with bold faith and ask for help. In Jesus' name. Amen.

For Jesus is not some high priest who has no sympathy for our weaknesses and flaws. He has already been tested in every way that we are tested; but He emerged victorious, without failing God. So let us step boldly to the throne of grace, where we can find mercy and grace to help when we need it most.
Hebrews 4:15-16 voice

TODAY'S FOCUS POINT

My strength is from God.

Graciously Forgiven

Father God, I confess this is hard for me to do. Forgiving someone for how they've wronged me feels like giving them a free pass. It feels like I'm invalidating the way they hurt me or letting them know it doesn't matter. Everything in me says to stand up for myself and hold them accountable. But then I remember what Jesus did on the cross and how it zeroed out my sins. I'm no longer held accountable, because I am forgiven. And I realize You're asking me to forgive because of it.

Let me take that revelation into my day, helping me release the gift of forgiveness to those who offend me. Rather than let anger fester into bitterness, I will forgive. Instead of keeping score of their wrongdoing, I will throw it away. Even more, God, let me do it graciously just as You did for me. In Jesus' name. Amen.

Tolerate the weaknesses of those in the family of faith,
forgiving one another in the same way you have been
graciously forgiven by Jesus Christ. If you find fault with
someone, release this same gift of forgiveness to them.
COLOSSIANS 3:13 TPT

TODAY'S FOCUS POINT

I don't have to live offended.

Giving Thanks in the Midst

Father God, show me how to make my life a prayer. Show me how to worship You each and every day with my attitude, words, and choices. Create in me a joy that's uncontainable and a faith that's anchored in a grateful heart. And let me be present and intentional to shine Your goodness into the world. Looking back, I see what an amazing Father You've been! I'm determined that my life reflect my unshakable gratitude for all You've done for me.

So let my focus throughout the day be on Your magnificence. Let me be quick to recognize Your hand moving in small and powerful ways when I'm in the middle of a mess. Help me remember that everything starts and ends with You because You're a God of detail. And let me find peace knowing Your plans for me and my family are perfect. In Jesus' name. Amen.

Let joy be your continual feast. Make your life a prayer.
And in the midst of everything be always giving thanks,
for this is God's perfect plan for you in Christ Jesus.
1 THESSALONIANS 5:16–18 TPT

TODAY'S FOCUS POINT

Be quick to thank God.

Shielded and Sheltered

Father God, today I'm feeling especially vulnerable. I've shared hard things with the right people. I've told the truth, even knowing it's unpopular. I've stood up for myself. I've stood up for what's right. And now I feel like I have a target on my back.

I'm praying today's verse over me right now. I know weapons have been fashioned against me already, but my prayer is that they don't succeed. Let my enemies' efforts fall flat. Keep them confused and uncoordinated. And let chaos run amok in their lives so they're distracted. I trust You to protect me through every challenging time because You promise to do so. So let me be courageous and confident, knowing You are shielding and sheltering me every day. In Jesus' name. Amen.

No weapon fashioned against you will succeed, and you may condemn every tongue that disputes with you. This is the heritage of the LORD's servants, whose righteousness comes from me, says the LORD.
ISAIAH 54:17 CEB

TODAY'S FOCUS POINT

No formed weapon will succeed.

Onto the Path of Peace

Father God, guide me onto the path of peace. My heart is tangled into knots as I try to navigate the beauty and heartache of life right now. In all the pain, there is beauty, but the pain is sometimes overwhelming. And honestly, there are times I feel stuck in it, unable to pull myself out. But You are a God of compassion. Your favor and grace will fall on me, illuminating the path of hope. In Your goodness, You will light up the path forward.

As I start my day, let me clearly see You. Open my eyes so I can follow You into a peaceful place where my heart can rest. I want to be effective today for my friends and family, and being stirred up in my spirit hinders that. So usher me into the light, speak encouragement to my soul, and lead me. In Jesus' name. Amen.

"Because of our God's deep compassion, the dawn from heaven will break upon us, to give light to those who are sitting in darkness and in the shadow of death, to guide us on the path of peace."
LUKE 1:78-79 CEB

TODAY'S FOCUS POINT

Stay on the path of peace.

Giving God Every Worry

Father God, today my burdens are heavy, and I'm worried about so many things. What I'd like to do is curl up in bed and hide for the day. I'd like to drown out the anxiety with a chick flick and some comfort food. And I'd like to talk about it over and over again with my bestie. But that's not what I'm going to do. Instead, I'm going to activate my faith and take You up on Your generous offer. I'm going to leave every burden at Your feet.

Lord, I know that when I do, there will be a supernatural exchange. I'll trade every one of my worries for Your perfect peace. I won't be shaken, because I'll be held tightly by You. And while I know I will face plenty of reasons to worry throughout my day, You'll always be my safe place. You're my sustainer. In Jesus' name. Amen.

Cast your burden on the LORD [release it] and He will sustain and uphold you; He will never allow the righteous to be shaken (slip, fall, fail).
PSALM 55:22 AMP

TODAY'S FOCUS POINT

Exchange my worries for His peace.

The Depth of His Protection

Father God, how wonderful to know that when I call out to You, some amazing things take place. Thank You that as I pray, an angel sets up a circle of protection around me. To realize that I'm protected in that moment—a moment of vulnerability—richly blesses me. It encourages me to embrace the moment rather than worry about the happenings around me. And then knowing You will protect me by getting me out of a tight spot brings relief.

As I venture out into the world today, let me stand confident in my relationship with You. Let me feel the blessing of Your presence in my life. Let me experience You with every one of my senses, praising You along the way. Your love and protection through Your hand and Your representative mean everything to me. In Jesus' name. Amen.

When I was desperate, I called out, and GOD got me out of a tight spot. GOD's angel sets up a circle of protection around us while we pray. Open your mouth and taste, open your eyes and see—how good GOD is. Blessed are you who run to him.
PSALM 34:6-8 MSG

TODAY'S FOCUS POINT

I'm protected as I pray.

When It Feels Overwhelming to Love

Father God, when I read today's verses I feel like a failure. Even on my best day, I cannot love this way. Even if it's the easiest-to-love person on the planet, I'm incapable of walking out today's verses well. I may be able to for a while, but at some point, my patience will wear thin. Show me how I can read this passage of scripture and feel encouraged.

Today, I am reminded that the goal of loving others isn't perfection. Thank You for that! Instead, I'm to be purposeful in how I care for others. And every day, I should be asking You to help me love them in meaningful ways that bless them. So let me find the right ways to love those around me so they are blessed. In Jesus' name. Amen.

Love is patient; love is kind. Love isn't envious, doesn't boast, brag, or strut about. There's no arrogance in love; it's never rude, crude, or indecent—it's not self-absorbed. Love isn't easily upset. Love doesn't tally wrongs or celebrate injustice; but truth—yes, truth—is love's delight!
1 Corinthians 13:4-6 voice

TODAY'S FOCUS POINT

I can love well with God's help.

Leaving Anxiety with God

Father God, I don't usually have trouble pouring out my worry and stress to You. As I go through my day, I'm quick to tell You about my anxiety. I love being able to share everything with You right then and there. And I am so grateful for Your listening ear that's always turned toward me. You're such a wonderful resource when I need to purge my feelings.

The problem is I often end up taking them back. Maybe it's because I want a quicker fix than what I see You doing. Maybe it's because I have a control issue. It all boils down to a lack of faith on my part. I need Your help so I can leave them in Your capable hands. There's nothing I can do that would ever trump Your perfect plan for hope and healing. So today, I'm going to let You be God, not me. And I'm going to enjoy the peace that comes from it. In Jesus' name. Amen.

Pour out all your worries and stress upon him and leave them there, for he always tenderly cares for you.
1 PETER 5:7 TPT

TODAY'S FOCUS POINT

Give all worries to God.

Peace over Confusion

Father God, what a timely reminder that You are not a God of confusion. Instead, You are the one who brings peace. You calm the tumultuous waters that threaten to toss me about. You create order out of chaos—be it in the world or in my heart. What I am desperate for right now—today—is for my heart to stop beating ninety miles an hour. I don't want to feel jittery because of stress. And I'm tired of feeling worn out all the time.

So bless me with peace! Let me have clarity of mind! Heal my heart. Restore my joy. Untangle any knots of fear and worry. Increase my faith. Help remove any unbelief. And let me operate in the knowledge of Your goodness every day. You are why I can stand strong when my life feels like a tornado. Lord, thank You for the gift of peace. In Jesus' name. Amen.

For He [Who is the source of their prophesying] is not a God of confusion and disorder but of peace and order. As [is the practice] in all the churches of the saints (God's people).
1 CORINTHIANS 14:33 AMPC

TODAY'S FOCUS POINT

Chaos and confusion are not from God.

Don't Let Worry Wander into Tomorrow

Father God, worry is a big deal in my life. It always has been. And it's not only my life that worries me but also what's happening in the lives of those I care about the most. This kind of fear keeps me up at night because I want everyone to be happy and healthy, even though I know that's not realistic. Too often, I look way down the road, and the potential outcomes I see are gnarly. What I predict is rarely good. But I want to think on what is true, and my worries aren't yet true.

Today, let me stay present as I trust You to bring clarity to each situation. I trust You to calm my heart. Even more, keep my worry from wandering into tomorrow. There's nothing good that will come from focusing on it. I know You're already there, straightening out each crooked path. So help me cling to that truth whenever I begin to feel my hope waver. In Jesus' name. Amen.

So do not worry or be anxious about tomorrow,
for tomorrow will have worries and anxieties of its
own. Sufficient for each day is its own trouble.
MATTHEW 6:34 AMPC

TODAY'S FOCUS POINT

Stay present in today.

Meeting Together

Father God, as the day of Jesus' return draws closer, today's verses ring very true in my heart. I can feel the need for community in my own life. I need—we all need—encouragement to be compassionate in a hard-hearted world. We need community to surround us so we feel encouraged to stand strong in our faith. And while I often want to hide away in response to all the craziness, that's not something I want to make a habit of.

Give me the energy and motivation to initiate get-togethers. It's so important to support one another, and doing that in person is the most powerful way. We all need a boost in our outlook. We need to be reminded of Your sovereignty. And together, we will find creative ways to meet the spiritual needs of each person. Help me facilitate this. In Jesus' name. Amen.

Discover creative ways to encourage others and to motivate them toward acts of compassion, doing beautiful works as expressions of love. This is not the time to pull away and neglect meeting together, as some have formed the habit of doing. In fact, we should come together even more frequently, eager to encourage and urge each other onward as we anticipate that day dawning.
HEBREWS 10:24–25 TPT

TODAY'S FOCUS POINT

Who should I connect with?

When Fear Drives Busyness

Father God, the truth is that sometimes my busyness is driven by fear. I think that the harder I work, the more likely it is that things will end up okay. I tell myself that working longer hours is key. And to work longer, I give up so much, like time with those I love. Rather than be present with my friends and family, my mind is always elsewhere.

I need You to remind me today that You see me and my circumstances. You know my every need and desire even before I do. You're already working things out for my benefit. And You are the giver of all good things, so I don't have to stay on that performance treadmill one more second. Scripture says You will provide even when I lay my head down to sleep! So settle my anxious heart and strengthen my faith so I don't waste my life with senseless toiling. In Jesus' name. Amen.

It really is senseless to work so hard from early morning till late at night, toiling to make a living for fear of not having enough. God can provide for his devoted lovers even while they sleep!
PSALM 127:2 TPT

TODAY'S FOCUS POINT

God will always provide!

A Dose of Divine Discernment

Father God, today I'm asking You for a dose of divine discernment. I tend to get so caught up in what the world says is good and right that I make the wrong choices. And those choices have natural consequences that are often frustrating and embarrassing. The problem is the things of this world are shiny. They glitter and sparkle and catch my eye. But they fail to satisfy for long.

Renew my mind as You transform my heart. I need a good old-fashioned house cleaning in my soul. When You get in there and refocus my attention on You rather than the world, I will be able to discern correctly. And in the end, I believe my choices will bless me and delight You. They will be full of things good and pleasing. In Jesus' name. Amen.

Do not allow this world to mold you in its own image. Instead, be transformed from the inside out by renewing your mind. As a result, you will be able to discern what God wills and whatever God finds good, pleasing, and complete.
ROMANS 12:2 VOICE

TODAY'S FOCUS POINT

Ask God for His discernment.

Confidence because of His Presence

Father God, I am beginning to see the connection between confidence and contentment. When I'm feeling *less than* or *not good enough*, I'll look for ways to change that. It may mean I use some retail therapy because buying things often makes me feel better. At least for a time. I may become obsessed with collecting stuff so I can keep up with those around me. But when I get caught up in that rat race, I miss the beautiful truth that it's Your presence that brings assurance.

Today, let me find confidence knowing I have the Creator with me. Let that truth be what bolsters my belief that I am good and worthy of love. I mean, if *You* want to be with me continually, then I must have value. In Jesus' name. Amen.

Don't be obsessed with getting more material things.
Be relaxed with what you have. Since God assured us,
"I'll never let you down, never walk off and leave you,"
we can boldly quote, God is there, ready to help; I'm
fearless no matter what. Who or what can get to me?
HEBREWS 13:5–6 MSG

TODAY'S FOCUS POINT

Material things don't build true confidence.

When Full of Despair

Father God, my feelings have been hurt. They've been stomped on then disregarded. And not only am I embarrassed but I'm also angry because this keeps happening. Why are people so unkind? Why does it seem they couldn't care less about being mean spirited? Why can't they see the harm they're inflicting? Today, I am tired of others being reckless with my heart and careless of how they treat it. Sometimes it may be accidental, but other times it's a deliberate act with full knowledge. And it stings deeply.

Scripture says You will bind up my wounds. What's more, it says You will heal the sorrows that tangle my heart. You alone are the great physician who promises to nurse my heart back to health. You will calm my anxiousness. You'll care for my emotional injuries. That means I can trust You to carefully tend every place of brokenness within me. In Your kindness, my feelings will be knit back together, and my sadness will fade away. I'll be able to let go of offenses because I will be aware of Your generous love. In Jesus' name. Amen.

He binds their wounds, heals the sorrows of their hearts.
PSALM 147:3 VOICE

TODAY'S FOCUS POINT

Ask God to heal my heart.

When I Feel Guilt

Father God, You know everything about me, and You still don't condemn me. You know about those seasons of sinning in my past. You see the ways I justify my sins today. You even have knowledge of the sins I'll commit in the future. Yes, You are fully aware of every wrongdoing—missteps that go against what I know to be good and right. And even then, You don't hold them over my head. No guilt comes from You. When I'm feeling it, it's self-condemnation.

Today I am asking for more awareness of Your presence in my life. Open the eyes of my heart so I can see You more clearly. Let me feel Your hand calming me when I begin pointing fingers at myself. Fill me with peace when I'm carrying the weight of the world on my shoulders. Bring me relief. In Jesus' name. Amen.

There is a sure way for us to know that we belong to the truth. Even though our inner thoughts may condemn us with storms of guilt and constant reminders of our failures, we can know in our hearts that in His presence God Himself is greater than any accusation. He knows all things.
1 JOHN 3:19-20 VOICE

TODAY'S FOCUS POINT

God isn't the source of my guilt.

Gratitude Each Step of the Way

Father God, thank You for guiding me through the ups and downs of life. You are with me when my relationships feel overwhelming and I'm not sure what to do next. You're with me when the bills are piling up. As I'm navigating life with a prodigal child, You're giving me wisdom and peace. When the test results are concerning, You are right there. And when there is reason to celebrate, You affirm my heart so I feel Your delight.

As I walk out the details of my life, let me do so with You on my mind. Let my words and actions reveal my faith as I trust You to intervene. Today, make my heart tender toward You as I remember Your promises to provide and to guide me. I want every detail of my day to glorify You. God, I'm filled with gratitude because You choose to weave Your love through my life. You've chosen to be in the details. And I'm so thankful. In Jesus' name. Amen.

Let every detail in your lives—words, actions,
whatever—be done in the name of the Master, Jesus,
thanking God the Father every step of the way.
COLOSSIANS 3:17 MSG

TODAY'S FOCUS POINT

Give God my gratitude.

God's Perfect Wisdom

Father God, Your wisdom is perfect and complex! It's multifaceted in the best of ways. And what a privilege to realize that when I ask, I can access it in my own life. I don't have to figure things out on my own. Instead, I can use Your wisdom, which is pure and peace loving. It's gentle, without harsh judgment. It's exact and doesn't waver on what's right or wrong. And it's straightforward so there's no confusion.

Today, would You bless me with Your steadfast wisdom? Let it give me confidence as I make decisions throughout my day. Let it make me courageous as I choose to follow Your leading. Let it be what steadies my heart when I feel confused or overwhelmed. Because I want to live a righteous life, let me live it through Your wisdom. In Jesus' name. Amen.

But the wisdom from above is first of all pure (undefiled); then it is peace-loving, courteous (considerate, gentle). [It is willing to] yield to reason, full of compassion and good fruits; it is wholehearted and straightforward, impartial and unfeigned (free from doubts, wavering, and insincerity).
JAMES 3:17 AMPC

TODAY'S FOCUS POINT

Ask God for His wisdom in all things.

Ornery or Obedient

Father God, thank You for calling me higher. The truth is that I'm often cantankerous. I've always had a bit of a rebellious streak in me, and I often do the opposite of what's asked. That is, when I'm operating in my flesh. When I'm not saturating my life in Your Word, I'm strong willed in all the wrong ways. I'm quickly irritated when asked to do something I don't feel like doing. And I'm sorry!

So today, help me see the blessing that comes from being obedient. Remind me that it delights Your heart, because that matters to me. And give me Your perspective on why following Your will and ways is good for me. I want to honor You with my life, and obeying Your commands does that. Even more, it brings me closer to You. So help me say yes to You rather than let my willfulness get me in trouble. In Jesus' name. Amen.

Let me give you some good advice; I'm looking you in the eye and giving it to you straight: "Don't be ornery like a horse or mule that needs bit and bridle to stay on track."
PSALM 32:8-9 MSG

TODAY'S FOCUS POINT

Obey God's plan for my day.

Anxious around Other Believers

Father God, community is a gift and something I should want in my life. Ministering together to the helpless and brokenhearted should be my desire. Being a part of Your church should delight my heart, making me feel connected to other believers in meaningful ways. Working in harmony to share Your Word should excite and energize me. But I confess today that I'm struggling.

I've been hurt by the church in the past and burned by believers. And it's made me anxious to join up with others. I love You, but sometimes I struggle with Your people. It's not that I'm in disharmony with them; I just don't invest. Please change my heart so I'm able to set those old hurts aside and reengage. Give me a desire to join together with others in Your name. In Jesus' name. Amen.

I pray that our God, who calls you and gives you perseverance and encouragement, will join all of you together to share one mind according to Jesus the Anointed. In this unity, you will share one voice as you glorify the one True God, the Father of our Lord Jesus, the Anointed One, our Liberating King.
ROMANS 15:5–6 VOICE

TODAY'S FOCUS POINT

God calls me to community.

Don't Be a Blabbermouth

Father God, You are going to have to help me with this! Too often, terrible words fly out of my mouth before I even realize it. I say mean things when I get defensive. When I see any injustice, I say things that don't glorify You. And when juicy gossip comes around, I waste no time sharing it. This is not how I want to live my life.

Will You start transforming my heart today? I don't want to be a blabbermouth about others, especially when bad things happen. There's no justification for passing along rumors, even under the guise of a prayer request. And whispering hearsay doesn't honor the one being discussed. Instead, help me use my words as beautiful gifts that encourage. Let them be laced with grace. And shut my mouth from sharing anything sensational or salacious about anyone. I don't want to be part of any rumor mill. In Jesus' name. Amen.

And never let ugly or hateful words come from your mouth, but instead let your words become beautiful gifts that encourage others; do this by speaking words of grace to help them.
EPHESIANS 4:29 TPT

TODAY'S FOCUS POINT

Make my words gifts of encouragement.

What You Hope For

Father God, what a relief to read today's verse and realize You have everything planned out. What a blessing to realize You really do know what You're doing in my life. This settles my spirit in significant ways because it reminds me that You are God and I am not. And thankfully, I don't have to be.

From the beginning, You've always had plans to take care of me. You have always cared about the desires of my heart. And long ago, You decided to stick with me and never walk away. In Your infinite wisdom, You created a path for my future that is full of. . .hope. So today, let me grab on to it with passion and purpose. Yes, I can confidently dream about what's ahead because You've already set it in motion. And when I share my hopes with You, letting You lead each step, good things are in store for me! In Jesus' name. Amen.

"I know what I'm doing. I have it all planned out—plans to take care of you, not abandon you, plans to give you the future you hope for."
JEREMIAH 29:11 MSG

TODAY'S FOCUS POINT

God knows what I hope for.

When Love Feels Unattainable

Father God, I often feel completely ill-equipped to love the way today's passage describes. It feels unattainable. It seems unreachable. And while I may be patient and gentle with someone one day, the next day I'm not. There may be one who doesn't irritate me—making them easy to love—but then another who always annoys me. Even being told to cheer someone on when I'm regularly jealous of their success is so hard.

But Father, I want to follow Your commands! I want to be a woman who loves over everything else. I want to be selfless and humble, ready to celebrate others with sincerity. And I know the only way I can find the grace and grit to do so is in Your strength. I can love this way because You first loved me. In Jesus' name. Amen.

Love is large and incredibly patient. Love is gentle and consistently kind to all. It refuses to be jealous when blessing comes to someone else. Love does not brag about one's achievements nor inflate its own importance. Love does not traffic in shame and disrespect, nor selfishly seek its own honor. Love is not easily irritated or quick to take offense.

1 CORINTHIANS 13:4–5 TPT

TODAY'S FOCUS POINT

I am able to love through God.

Always an Attitude of Praise

Father God, I confess there are lots of reasons for the bad attitude I sometimes exhibit. When life hits hard, I get cranky from being overwhelmed by my mess. My rebellious spirit sometimes gets me into trouble, especially when I'm told I must do something (even if it's for You). And other times I'm just not in the mood to be cheerful and happy. Thank You for loving me in my wretchedness! And forgive me.

Today, my heart's desire is to embrace a better attitude no matter what the circumstances surrounding my life may be. Regardless of my mood or mess, let me always be ready and willing to offer up a sacrifice of praise to You! Let my words recognize Your goodness. Let them glorify who You are to me. And let me find reasons to be grateful even in the tough spaces, because there are always reasons to praise You! In Jesus' name. Amen.

Through Him, therefore, let us at all times offer up to God a sacrifice of praise, which is the fruit of lips that thankfully acknowledge and confess and glorify His name.
HEBREWS 13:15 AMP

TODAY'S FOCUS POINT

Praise God at all times!

Trusting God to Guide

Father God, thank You for promising to guide me as I navigate the ups and downs of this life. Sometimes I am conflicted on what to do next, and I honestly don't know what the best road forward is. The last thing I want is to make a wrong turn that leaves me in a messy situation. I don't want to make snap decisions that lead me to bad places. And I don't want to choose on my own because You see the big picture while I cannot.

Allow me to hear You in my spirit, Lord. Bless me with spiritual eyes and ears so I can follow as You lead me. Give me a confident faith that trusts that You will course correct if I've heard Your plans incorrectly. And let me always seek Your wisdom for the next step rather than follow the crowd or trust my instincts. In Jesus' name. Amen.

Your ears will hear sweet words behind you: "Go this way. There is your path; this is how you should go" whenever you must decide whether to turn to the right or the left.
ISAIAH 30:21 VOICE

TODAY'S FOCUS POINT

Look and listen for God's leading.

Sometimes Distractions Are Good

Father God, I have often felt sorry for Martha in today's passage of scripture because I know what it feels like to be abandoned. Many times I've been the one left to do the work while others enjoyed being together. I've been in the kitchen alone, missing out on fellowship and making sure everyone else is taken care of. And it's built up resentment in my heart. Then I see it from another perspective.

Lord, I want to be more like Mary. She understood what was important and allowed herself to be distracted by it. Help me not be so rigid that I miss You. Don't let my calendar keep me from making time for You. Today, keep my heart from being hard so I'm willing to forgo my to-do list to walk out Your will. In Jesus' name. Amen.

She had a sister named Mary, who sat at the Lord's feet and listened to his message. By contrast, Martha was preoccupied with getting everything ready for their meal. So Martha came to him and said, "Lord, don't you care that my sister has left me to prepare the table all by myself? Tell her to help me."
LUKE 10:39–40 CEB

TODAY'S FOCUS POINT

Prioritize God above all else.

The Favor of the Lord

Father God, if You aren't with me today, I don't want to take another step. I don't want to put my hands and mind to work if what I'm doing isn't blessed by You. I am desperate to stay in Your will and follow Your ways for my life. The beauty, the delightfulness, the favor that comes from You is what fuels me forward. And so today, let me know You're with me and for me.

Let my life be a gift to You and a blessing to others. I have no desire to go it alone and hope for the best. I want to do what You created me to do. And even though I can't audibly hear Your voice, I do feel You speaking to my heart. Father, in Your graciousness, please direct me in Your ways. Confirm in me Your plans for my life and then establish them by Your favor. I'm all in, but my heart desires confirmation. Would You give me that today? In Jesus' name. Amen.

And let the beauty and delightfulness and favor of the Lord our God be upon us; confirm and establish the work of our hands—yes, the work of our hands, confirm and establish it.
PSALM 90:17 AMPC

TODAY'S FOCUS POINT

Follow the favor of God.

Fear in the Valleys

Father God, it's hard to imagine walking through the valley of the deepest darkness and not being afraid. That valley is full of unknowns. It's hard to see the path forward. I feel so alone, trying to feel my way around. And I'm just waiting for something to jump out and scare me. It's destabilizing and uncomfortable. That is, when I'm walking without You.

But what I love is that when I do cling to You in those rough seasons, they are uncharacteristically sweet. There is something beautiful about times of long-suffering with You next to me. I never feel closer to my Father than when I am holding on for dear life. My fear melts away as I sense Your goodness and presence with me. I feel held. And right there with You is exactly where I want to be. In Jesus' name. Amen.

*Even when your path takes me through the valley
of deepest darkness, fear will never conquer me,
for you already have! Your authority is my strength
and my peace. The comfort of your love takes away
my fear. I'll never be lonely, for you are near.*
PSALM 23:4 TPT

TODAY'S FOCUS POINT

God always lights up the darkness.

When the World Stirs Up Insecurity

Father God, I've noticed that when I focus on what the world says is good and right, my insecurities flare up. That's when I begin to compare myself to people's standards and I never measure up. . .at least not for long. Their definition of beauty changes all the time. What they consider important rarely aligns with what You say is important. And I'm watching them twist what I know to be godly into something unrecognizable. In the end, it leaves me feeling terrible.

So today I'm choosing to set the affections of my heart on You alone. God, I want You to know that Your Word matters to me. What You say is not only powerful but also transformative. It's my heart's desire to stand strong in things eternal and not temporal. I love You above all else. Let my life be living proof of it. And keep me from thinking the grass is greener over there because I'm firmly rooted in You! In Jesus' name. Amen.

Don't set the affections of your heart on this world or in loving the things of the world. The love of the Father and the love of the world are incompatible.
1 JOHN 2:15 TPT

TODAY'S FOCUS POINT

Love God more than the world.

Obedience to God's Word

Father God, help me be eager not only to hear Your Word but also to walk it out each day. I confess the times I've been deeply moved by scripture in one moment but then forgot it in the next. I confess the times I've run across a well-timed verse but failed to put it into action. Forgive me for treating the Word so carelessly.

God, You say I will be blessed when I guard Your Word in my heart. Choosing to stand strong and believe the Bible even in the hardest times will be seen as an act of obedience in Your eyes. Clinging to my favorite verses in the darkest valleys will reap rewards because I trusted You more than I feared the unknown. So bless me today as I ruminate on Your Word in my heart. As I navigate the difficulties of my day, watch my faith rise up in strength because my heart is focused on the mighty words from the Bible. In Jesus' name. Amen.

Jesus commented, "Even more blessed are those who hear God's Word and guard it with their lives!"
LUKE 11:28 MSG

TODAY'S FOCUS POINT

Cherish God's Word in my heart.

It's All about Faith

Father God, it's such a relief to know there is nothing I can do to earn my salvation. Thank You for not leaving it up to me! I am foolish and wretched, and I'd never want my actions to be what determines my place in heaven. I simply could never make it there if left to my own devices.

So this morning I find myself so thankful for Your grace. It's Your love that has made it possible to live with You forever. Jesus' death on the cross paid my sin debt, allowing me to stand blameless in Your sight. And my belief in this beautiful redemption—my faith in You—has opened the door to heaven. It's all You, God. I take no glory for myself. Eternity isn't a reward for my good deeds. It's a blessing that results from my faith. I love You so much! In Jesus' name. Amen.

For by grace you have been saved by faith. Nothing you did could ever earn this salvation, for it was the love gift from God that brought us to Christ! So no one will ever be able to boast, for salvation is never a reward for good works or human striving.
EPHESIANS 2:8-9 TPT

TODAY'S FOCUS POINT

I can't earn my way to heaven.

Peace in Every Circumstance

Father God, today's verse has powerfully settled my heart this morning. Thank You for knowing not only the perfect scriptures to include in Your Word, but also the exact time we need to read them. I'm so grateful You know everything we need and choose to bless us abundantly.

I've been so unsettled because life isn't going how I had hoped. What I had planned for hasn't panned out. Where I thought I'd be right now isn't here. And even those I love have decided to walk some difficult paths I prayed they never would. But here we are. What's more, the world seems so crazy right now and sometimes brings out fear and worry. So to read that You will pour Your peace into *every* circumstance and in *every* possible way means everything to me. Calm me today, Lord. May Your peace and presence bring overwhelming relief to my spirit. In Jesus' name. Amen.

> *May the Lord of peace give you His peace*
> *at all times. The Lord be with you all.*
> 2 Thessalonians 3:16 nlv

TODAY'S FOCUS POINT

I can feel peace no matter what.

Only Wanting God's Approval

Father God, set my heart in such a way that You are all I crave. Give me a deep love for You over anything this world may offer. Help me navigate being in this world but not of it. I don't want to fit in here. I don't want to find comfort here. And I don't ever want to align myself with what it offers. Being part of this world's system does nothing but corrupt my heart, keeping it focused on all the wrong things.

Today, turn every affection of mine toward You. I want to live in peace with You, Father. When my heart lines up with the world's offering it's considered warring against You, and knowing that encourages me to look only for Your approval. Lord, all I want is more of You. Let that be apparent in how I choose to live my life. In Jesus' name. Amen.

You are adulterers. Don't you know that making friends with this corrupt world order is open aggression toward God? So anyone who aligns with this bogus world system is declaring war against the one true God.
JAMES 4:4 VOICE

TODAY'S FOCUS POINT

The world holds nothing for me.

Weak Moments

Father God, what a beautiful shift in perspective! For most of my life, I've believed that weakness was a bad thing. I thought it made me *less than* others. I worried it made me unattractive. But as Your Word so profoundly points out in today's scripture, my weakness is worthy of my delight! Why? Because it's in my weak moments that Your power is on display. When there's no way I should be standing in the storm, it's Your might flowing through me that reveals Your greatness.

Rather than remain focused on my feebleness, I can celebrate that it's what ushers in Your muscle. I don't need to be in control because I believe You are. I trust You to hold me up during the hard seasons. You're why I can persevere. So as I go through my day, let me rejoice in Your power made perfect in my weak moments. In Jesus' name. Amen.

*So I'm not defeated by my weakness, but delighted!
For when I feel my weakness and endure
mistreatment—when I'm surrounded with troubles
on every side and face persecution because of my
love for Christ—I am made yet stronger. For my
weakness becomes a portal to God's power.*

2 CORINTHIANS 12:10 TPT

TODAY'S FOCUS POINT

It's God who strengthens me.

Remembering to Worship

Father God, today I'm going to intentionally think back to the glorious things I've seen You do in my life and in the lives of those I love. You have demonstrated Your compassion in magnificent ways, and I'm going to meditate on them throughout my day. And from my time of remembering, I will worship who You are and all You've done to love Your children.

I recall countless times You intervened when my situation looked bleak, and hope sprang forth. You've course corrected me more than once, setting me back on the path You lovingly created. I've had money show up just in time. I've seen disease and health concerns disappear altogether. You've brought beauty from ashes and joy from grief. In my hardest moments, You have pulled me from despair when I wanted to sit in self-pity. Yes, Father, You have done excellent and glorious things. Let me be quick to share my testimony with the world! In Jesus' name. Amen.

Sing praises to the LORD, for He has done excellent and glorious things; let this be known throughout the earth.
ISAIAH 12:5 AMP

TODAY'S FOCUS POINT

Praise God for His goodness!

Empowered in Weakness

Father God, I love knowing that in my weakness, You will empower me. Because honestly, I feel weak so much these days. I often struggle to make decisions, unsure of what the best answer is. When life is overwhelming and I'm drained, I just want to curl up in bed and hide under the covers. Physically, my body is aging, and I don't have the strength and dexterity I once had when I was younger. Spiritually, I feel weak when I give in to temptation, especially because I know better.

So strengthen me—every part of me. Toughen me up emotionally and spiritually, giving me the resolve to do what I know is right. Help me know what to pray when I'm struggling to stand strong in the face of adversity. And let the Holy Spirit intercede when my grit dwindles. Today, I need Your muscle. In Jesus' name. Amen.

And in a similar way, the Holy Spirit takes hold of us in our human frailty to empower us in our weakness. For example, at times we don't even know how to pray, or know the best things to ask for. But the Holy Spirit rises up within us to super-intercede on our behalf, pleading to God with emotional sighs too deep for words.

ROMANS 8:26 TPT

TODAY'S FOCUS POINT

God will fortify me with His strength.

God Always Provides

Father God, thank You for being the kind of Father who blesses those who follow Him. When I am trying to walk out my faith with integrity—even when I mess up royally—You bless me richly through Your unmatched provision. And You give lavishly, leaving me feeling the fullness of Your delight.

As I start my day, would You meet those needs that often go unmet? Cover me with Your grace to navigate the hard conversations. Wrap around me like a shield, protecting my heart from the enemy's arrows that aim to hurt my feelings. Shine brightly into my spirit so I feel energized for what lies ahead. And be generous with me so my cup runneth over and I can pass that generosity along to others. Thank You for providing for me in beautiful and powerful ways. In Jesus' name. Amen.

For the Lord God is brighter than the brilliance of a sunrise! Wrapping himself around me like a shield, he is so generous with his gifts of grace and glory. Those who walk along his paths with integrity will never lack one thing they need, for he provides it all!

PSALM 84:11 TPT

TODAY'S FOCUS POINT

God will meet every need I have.

Craving God's Favor

Father God, the world today seems very much like the times of Noah. Sometimes I don't know how You stand it one second longer. People are trying to remove Your holy name from buildings and institutions. The way You intended families and marriages to exist is in question. And we can no longer have healthy conversations and disagreements because deep lines have been drawn in the sand. Forgive us!

Here is my request today. Lord, let me be like Noah in Your eyes. Let my life honor You in significant ways so You're blessed by how I live. Give me words to express Your magnificence. Help me be confident in my faith so I always trust You. And help me make the right choices every day so I'll feel Your favor resting on me. I crave Your approval. In Jesus' name. Amen.

So the LORD said, "I will wipe off of the land the human race that I've created: from human beings to livestock to the crawling things to the birds in the skies, because I regret I ever made them." But as for Noah, the LORD approved of him.
GENESIS 6:7–8 CEB

TODAY'S FOCUS POINT

Make choices that please God.

What Are You Focusing On?

Father God, scripture talks about the importance of choosing the right things to fill our minds with. It's detailed about what we should focus our attention on. And I'm so thankful for the reminder today because I've been letting my thought life run wild lately, and I realize it may be the reason for my anxiety.

When I'm in the Word daily and meditating on Your words, my heart is settled. My life may be chaotic, but the Bible encourages me in unparalleled ways and I'm able to thrive no matter what. As I walk into my day, help me think about what is right and pure and lovely. Help me ruminate on what is good and praiseworthy. There's no better way to relieve stress and be strengthened. In Jesus' name. Amen.

Finally, brothers and sisters, fill your minds with beauty and truth. Meditate on whatever is honorable, whatever is right, whatever is pure, whatever is lovely, whatever is good, whatever is virtuous and praiseworthy. Keep to the script: whatever you learned and received and heard and saw in me—do it—and the God of peace will walk with you.
PHILIPPIANS 4:8-9 VOICE

TODAY'S FOCUS POINT

Fill my mind with God's truth.

Blaming God for Hardships

Father God, I confess there are times I am so overwhelmed by the struggles I'm facing that I get angry at You. Rather than remind myself that every hardship is Father filtered and full of purpose, I begin asking the wrong questions. *Why did You allow this? Am I being punished? Aren't You supposed to be protecting me?*

Today, help me remember that You're always at work in my circumstances. While it may not feel that way in the moment, I know I can trust You fully and completely. What's more, scripture says it's a privilege to share in Christ's sufferings! And I know You will use every tough situation to refine my faith. Help me stand strong in these storms as I wait for You rather than give in to despair. I know You've got me. In Jesus' name. Amen.

Friends, when life gets really difficult, don't jump to the conclusion that God isn't on the job. Instead, be glad that you are in the very thick of what Christ experienced. This is a spiritual refining process, with glory just around the corner.
1 Peter 4:12-13 MSG

TODAY'S FOCUS POINT

God is always working on my behalf.

The Power of Kindness

Father God, I want my life to count. I want to spend today and every day living and loving others well. Soften my heart so it breaks for the poor. Fill me with compassion for the widow and orphan. Give me the spiritual eyes to see the needs of the downtrodden. And nudge me when someone is hurting so I can meet them there, ready to tell them of Your love and goodness.

My life is full, and I can be so focused on myself that I miss others along the way. The truth is I have work and family and friends to honor. I have other commitments that take up time and energy. But God, I don't ever want to be so overloaded with life that I can't share kindness with those around me. Please don't let my heart harden in that way. Instead, bless me with supernatural insight so I'll know when someone is desperate for a kind act or a compassionate moment. In Jesus' name. Amen.

Whoever cares for the poor makes a loan to the Eternal;
such kindness will be repaid in full and with interest.
PROVERBS 19:17 VOICE

TODAY'S FOCUS POINT

Who needs an act of kindness?

Seeing the Vulnerable

Father God, help me respect the vulnerability of others today. Because I know how painful and challenging it can be to reveal hard things, let me be a safe space when necessary. Let me be someone whom others can confide in with confidence, trusting me with difficult details. Let my words be full of truth and grace without any hint of criticism. And allow me favor to say what needs to be said while caring for people at the same time.

Will You also fill me with compassion for the oppressed? Will You bless me with the ability to see them in their vulnerability and understand their unique needs? In each situation, give me broad shoulders to help them walk the tough road. We all need the gift of community. And I know I'm not above serving anyone who is in a rough season. In Jesus' name. Amen.

Live creatively, friends. If someone falls into sin, forgivingly restore him, saving your critical comments for yourself. You might be needing forgiveness before the day's out. Stoop down and reach out to those who are oppressed. Share their burdens, and so complete Christ's law. If you think you are too good for that, you are badly deceived.
GALATIANS 6:1–3 MSG

TODAY'S FOCUS POINT

Give me compassion for the vulnerable.

Worshipping in Awe

Father God, I'm blown away by the unmistakable ways You've shown up in my life. You've demonstrated love in such tangible ways! When I think about how You restored relationships that were deeply broken, I'm in awe. You've provided financially when I was in serious and immediate trouble. I've seen You heal broken bones and broken hearts and broken lives. You have opened the right doors and closed the wrong ones, repeatedly. And I've seen hard hearts soften through Your patient and loving care. I say bravo, God, bravo! Don't stop now!

Starting today, may my life choices demonstrate the commitment I've made to follow You. Until my last breath, I will praise Your name and share my testimony of Your generosity. I will talk about Your goodness to all who will listen. And it will be my honor to worship You through my faith, overwhelmed by Your visible power. In Jesus' name. Amen.

Bravo, GOD, bravo! Gods and all angels shout, "Encore!"
In awe before the glory, in awe before God's visible
power. Stand at attention! Dress your best to honor him!
PSALM 29:1-2 MSG

TODAY'S FOCUS POINT

Worship God for His unwavering faithfulness.

Being Extremely Thankful

Father God, let my life offer You the purest kind of worship. In every choice I make, let my desire to please You shine through. Check and see that my motives are untainted. My heart's desire is to delight You by the words I speak and the actions I take because I'm just so grateful for the ways You've shown me kindness. So, thank You for Your generosity. And thank You for Your faithfulness in my life.

Your unshakable kingdom is my final destination thanks to Your Son's death on the cross. He made a way for me to live forever with You in eternity. Today, I fully surrender to Your will and ways. My life is Yours, now and always. And I'm praising Your holy name with fervor. As I think back to the times You've intervened in my circumstances, my heart is full and I'm extremely thankful. In Jesus' name. Amen.

Since we are receiving our rights to an unshakable
kingdom we should be extremely thankful and offer
God the purest worship that delights his heart as we lay
down our lives in absolute surrender, filled with awe.
HEBREWS 12:28 TPT

TODAY'S FOCUS POINT

Let God see my gratitude.

God's Strength against Temptation

Father God, it's good to know that no matter what temptations come my way, I will have the strength necessary to escape them. They won't overpower me when my resolve comes from You. It may not always feel like it in the moment, but I will be able to endure the stress and strain of them. I'll have the grit to keep moving forward, thanks to Your provision.

What's more, You know my limits. And that means I won't be tempted in ways that make me unable to stand strong. In faith, I may bend but I won't break under the pressure of temptation. I know my weaknesses, just as the enemy does. The playbook isn't new. So today, I'm trusting Your words and Your faithfulness. I'm believing that You will strengthen me so I can live victoriously! In Jesus' name. Amen.

Any temptation you face will be nothing new. But God is faithful, and He will not let you be tempted beyond what you can handle. But He always provides a way of escape so that you will be able to endure and keep moving forward.
1 CORINTHIANS 10:13 VOICE

TODAY'S FOCUS POINT

Every temptation has an escape route.

Never Separated

Father God, what a relief to realize nothing I do has the capability to separate me from You. When I am in happy seasons and I unknowingly push You into last place, thank You for not walking away. When my insecurities take over and I cling to control with all my might instead of looking for Your help, thank You for sticking close. And when my choices lead me in the wrong direction and I hide in shame, thank You for loving me anyway.

Sometimes in my hardships, I push You away because I feel ashamed. I think You may be mad at me for my wrongdoing. So today, let the life-giving words from Romans comfort me. Speak these powerful truths into the darkest parts of my heart. And let me bloom, knowing I'm safe and secure with You. No matter what—be it in the easy or the hard—I am Yours forever. In Jesus' name. Amen.

So now I live with the confidence that there is nothing in the universe with the power to separate us from God's love. I'm convinced that his love will triumph over death, life's troubles, fallen angels, or dark rulers in the heavens. There is nothing in our present or future circumstances that can weaken his love.
ROMANS 8:38 TPT

TODAY'S FOCUS POINT

Nothing can ever separate me from God.

Even When Bad Things Happen

Father God, I know hardships are just a part of the human experience. I understand they are something every one of us will face. The truth is that You never promised an easy, carefree life. You never told us things would be easy-peasy. And nowhere in Your Word does it set us up to believe our time here on earth will be a cakewalk. Instead, the Bible is very clear about the reality we'll face as we navigate this life.

But what I so love and appreciate about You is that these hard moments won't take me out. When I place my trust in You alone, there is great provision. There is promised restoration. There is detailed healing. There is unwavering love. Nothing on earth can defeat me because You stand between me and every single hardship. My faith is made even stronger as I watch You create a way through the valleys. In Jesus' name. Amen.

*Even when bad things happen to the good and
godly ones, the Lord will save them and not
let them be defeated by what they face.*
PSALM 34:19 TPT

TODAY'S FOCUS POINT

There is no defeat with God.

When I'm on Worry Overload

Father God, help me. I'm having the hardest time keeping worry under control. I feel anxious every morning and it carries through the day. I feel stressed out most of the time, concerned with how things are going to turn out. And nighttime is tough because I can't stop my mind from running ninety miles an hour. Today I am struggling, and the load is heavy for my heart.

Scripture is clear when it says You will give me rest; You will exchange my burden for Your yoke because it's easy and light. Lord, I'm asking for that right now. Lift this heaviness off me as I lean into You for help. Calm my anxiousness so I'm able to be effective and engaged in my life. And keep me close so I feel Your presence, for that's what ushers in peace and comfort. Thank You for taking care of me in such meaningful ways. In Jesus' name. Amen.

*"Come to me, all you who are struggling hard
and carrying heavy loads, and I will give you rest.
Put on my yoke, and learn from me. I'm gentle and
humble. And you will find rest for yourselves.
My yoke is easy to bear, and my burden is light."*
MATTHEW 11:28–30 CEB

TODAY'S FOCUS POINT

God wants my every worry.

Eternal Perspective

Father God, help me remember in my pursuit of stuff that I can't take any of it with me when I go to heaven. The fancy clothes and the cool home decor and newest electronic gadgets stay here. When I see You face-to-face, none of it will have transferred up. So Lord, why am I so obsessed with getting more? Why do I have to have the latest and greatest?

Today, give me an eternal perspective on what's important. Let me recognize the things that are truly important during my time on earth. Remind me of what I can pursue now that has heavenly benefits. That's where I want my focus to be. That's what I'm interested in chasing after. Help me love well, forgive often, serve others, show compassion, and bless You with my life. Let my contentment rest in lofty places over any worldly offering. In Jesus' name. Amen.

This is ironic because godliness, along with contentment, does put us ahead but not in the ways some imagine. You see we came into this world with nothing, and nothing is going with us on the way out! So as long as we are clothed and fed, we should be happy.
1 TIMOTHY 6:6–8 VOICE

TODAY'S FOCUS POINT

Find contentment in eternal things.

An Attitude That Shines

Father God, help my attitude today. Sometimes I just get cranky and see everything in a negative light. The truth is that I don't always want to adult! So rather than be respectful and responsible, I grumble. I complain to anyone who will listen. And I behave in a graceless manner—quick to snap at those who get in my way or challenge my mood. God, who wants to be around someone like that?!

Deep down, what I really want is to shine Your goodness into the lives of others. I want to live in such a way that others see You radiate from the inside out. As a believer, my greatest desire is for You to have transformed my heart in such a way that it's noticeable, and as a result it opens the door for me to share my faith. So help my attitude reflect that hope. Let me shine like a star in the world. In Jesus' name. Amen.

Do everything without grumbling and arguing so that you may be blameless and pure, innocent children of God surrounded by people who are crooked and corrupt. Among these people you shine like stars in the world.
PHILIPPIANS 2:14–15 CEB

TODAY'S FOCUS POINT

Be a light in the grumbling world.

Growing through the Hardships

Father God, from childhood, the world has conditioned me to look at my hardships in a negative light. It's encouraged me to take inventory, to look at choices I've made that might have caused the problems I'm working through. Some have told me it's karma or payback. They say I brought it on myself, which only makes me feel guilty or ashamed. But today's verses help me see my struggles differently! I realize that regardless of what brought them on, You are working on me through them. They have purpose.

While I don't welcome hardships or find myself excited when they cross my path, I'm so grateful to know You're at work in them. Tough times don't have to take me out, like in the past. Now, I can faithfully embrace them, trusting You not only to help me through but also to grow me through. From endurance to character to hope—what a blessing to know You waste nothing! That revelation is marvelous. In Jesus' name. Amen.

But not only that! We even take pride in our problems, because we know that trouble produces endurance, endurance produces character, and character produces hope.
Romans 5:3-4 CEB

TODAY'S FOCUS POINT

Problems present growth opportunities.

Persevering for What's Right

Father God, Your promise is clear. And it provides such a powerful incentive to press into You for strength when life gets hard. My faith should shine the brightest when I need that extra push to get over the finish line, because as I rely on You, I'm able to straighten my back and stand tall. I can find courage to continue. I can see hope on the horizon. And I realize nothing is impossible when I'm trusting You!

So today, please strengthen me for what lies ahead. Give me wisdom to endure the tough moments I will inevitably face. Sustain me as I cling to You for guidance and support. Enable me to stay focused and energized to do the right thing. God, I realize that to suffer without You would be unbearable. It would keep me stuck in the bondage of hopelessness. Keep me on track so I can experience the blessing that will follow. In Jesus' name. Amen.

May we never tire of doing what is good and right
before our Lord because in His season we shall
bring in a great harvest if we can just persist.
GALATIANS 6:9 VOICE

TODAY'S FOCUS POINT

I can persevere through anything with God.

Hidden Jealousy

Father God, I recognize that when I keep things hidden in the dark, they fester. It's the enemy's playground, and it's where lies become tangled up. I've seen this at work firsthand throughout my life. I know the best plan for hidden sin is to expose it to the light, even if it's uncomfortable and scary. For You to heal it, You must reveal it.

Today, jealousy is a real issue in my life. I find myself— sometimes without realizing it—comparing my lack to the abundance of others. I notice what they have and what they do. I see how their family seems to be thriving. I see how their marriage looks perfect. So often, I find myself too aware of my don't-haves and the result is a jealous heart. Remove it from me, Lord, and replace it with a heart of gratitude for all I do have. In Jesus' name. Amen.

But if there is bitter jealousy or competition hiding in your heart, then don't deny it and try to compensate for it by boasting and being phony. For that has nothing to do with God's heavenly wisdom but can best be described as the wisdom of this world, both selfish and devilish.

JAMES 3:14–15 TPT

TODAY'S FOCUS POINT

I'm content with what I have.

The God of Provision

Father God, let today's verse calm my anxious heart and strengthen my faith in You. You're a God who consistently and generously provides for His children. And because I fall into that category, I can find relief knowing Your provision includes me too. I don't need to worry about my basic needs because You're on the throne and in full control. You see my situation clearly and fully. So quiet my spirit and settle my heart.

I've been carrying this burden for too long. I've been trying to make all the ends meet in my own strength. And I'm tired and frustrated, filled with feelings of hopelessness. In Your kindness, would You take that burden from me today? Would You exchange it for Your yoke, which is light and easy? And help me remember that I'm not my own savior; Jesus is. My hope and trust are now anchored in You alone. In Jesus' name. Amen.

Every living thing that moves will be available to you as food. Just as I once gave you the green plants to eat, I now give you everything.
GENESIS 9:3 VOICE

TODAY'S FOCUS POINT

God will provide.

Happy in the Hardships

Father God, I know Your Word says there are blessings in store for me if I can hold up under the trials of life. But I also know that's not easy to do. There are times when I'd rather hide under the covers and suck my thumb than face what's coming. Life can hit hard and it's always unfair, and there are moments it catches me off guard.

My desire is to have a steady, unshakable heart through the tough times. I don't want to be tossed about, because it does nothing but destabilize me emotionally. Let my faith mature so I can live with a victory mindset, trusting that You will work all things out for my good. That alone will bring me joy and happiness. And with the understanding that Your approval comes from standing strong, today I am resolved to live in such a way. Thank You for Your promises. In Jesus' name. Amen.

Happy is the person who can hold up under the trials of life. At the right time, he'll know God's sweet approval and will be crowned with life. As God has promised, the crown awaits all who love Him.
JAMES 1:12 VOICE

TODAY'S FOCUS POINT

Standing strong brings godly blessings.

When Vulnerability Feels Hard

Father God, help me choose to be vulnerable today. I know it's a choice that isn't always easy to make. Sometimes it feels easier to just stay closed off. Sometimes it's easier to keep the depths of my heart hidden. Lots of times, it feels safer that way. But creating intimacy in community requires honest modesty. It means I have the courage to let others see the warts in my life. It means I'm willing to share the ugly parts of my struggles. There's no better way to grow deeper than to just be real.

But God, please also give me discernment to know who I can trust. I want to be wise about who I tell, because there are some people who may take advantage of my openness. I trust You to bless me with the perfect group of friends to walk through the ups and downs of life with! In Jesus' name. Amen.

So own up to your sins to one another and pray for one another. In the end, you may be healed. Your prayers are powerful when they are rooted in a righteous life.
JAMES 5:16 VOICE

TODAY'S FOCUS POINT

It's okay to be honest with the right people.

Trusting God Enough to Surrender

Father God, today I surrender my life into Your hands. Honestly, it isn't easy to relinquish that kind of control. I've been burned so many times by allowing others to make decisions for me, and I'm a little shy about it. And even though You are God, flawless and perfect in every way, it's not easy to let go of the wheel. But today I am choosing to believe what Your Word says. I am trusting You. Be gentle with my heart.

Here's what I know to be true of You, God. Your heart for me is always good and Your love is unshakable. You're unable to break promises made—whether the ones in Your Word or the ones spoken into my heart. You know me better than I know myself and understand the complexity of my situations. And You have a hope-filled future waiting for me. Knowing this, I ask You to encourage my heart to trust You fully and completely. In Jesus' name. Amen.

Give God the right to direct your life, and as you trust him along the way, you'll find he pulled it off perfectly!
PSALM 37:5 TPT

TODAY'S FOCUS POINT

I can trust God with every situation.

I Just Wanna Say Thanks

Father God, forgive me for times I've not been grateful for the help You've provided. You deserve praise for the ways You love me so completely. Because You are always with me and for me, words of thanksgiving should be the first ones out of my mouth. I'm sorry they're not. And it's something I want to change.

Rather than rattle off a lengthy list of needs and wants, today I simply want to spend time thanking You. I remember how You restored some particularly important relationships. I saw how You healed my broken heart a time or two. I watched You change hearts of stone, filling them with love and compassion. God, thank You for being kind and generous to me and those I care about. I appreciate the ways You have stood in my corner when I felt alone and hopeless. And I'm glad I can lean on You at any time, confident You'll hear and respond in the best ways for my situation. You're amazing. In Jesus' name. Amen.

Be persistent and devoted to prayer, being alert and focused in your prayer life with an attitude of thanksgiving.
COLOSSIANS 4:2 AMP

TODAY'S FOCUS POINT

God, thank You for everything.

Supernaturally Infused Strength

Father God, I realize it's because I am a believer that I'm able to be infused with Your strength. You're why I can stand up for what's right. You are why I'm able to be bold with my words. Because my faith is in You, I can find the muscle to navigate whatever comes my way with a victory mindset. It's not in my strength, but in Yours coursing through my veins.

Too often, I default to my own strength. I trust in my own skills. So God, supernaturally impart power to me today. I want Yours over mine! Help me be courageous in the places where I need to be. Make me confident as I trust that You will give me what is necessary to advocate with gusto. Remove fear that tries to render me helpless. I may not know how the victory will come, but I trust it will. In Jesus' name. Amen.

Now my beloved ones, I have saved these most important truths for last: Be supernaturally infused with strength through your life-union with the Lord Jesus. Stand victorious with the force of his explosive power flowing in and through you.
EPHESIANS 6:10 TPT

TODAY'S FOCUS POINT

Let God strengthen me.

The Beautiful Gift of Kindness

Father God, I've often heard it said that in a world where you can be anything, be kind. Not only does being kind benefit me and glorify You, but it brings beautiful blessings into the lives of others. It tells someone they are worthy of good things. It adds a pep in their step. And it can change the entire trajectory of their day. Kindness is the new cool.

In the same vein, help me also be kind in my instruction. Be it toward my children, my friends, or those who look up to me for wisdom, allow kindness to flow through my words in fresh and meaningful ways. Even when what I need to say is hard to hear and harder to digest, let me be mindful of the words I choose to speak. Prepare my heart so the fullness overflows and is well received. And allow my words to have the desired impact, sparking someone into action or settling their spirit. God, may You always be glorified. In Jesus' name. Amen.

Her teachings are filled with wisdom and kindness
as loving instruction pours from her lips.
PROVERBS 31:26 TPT

TODAY'S FOCUS POINT

Share wisdom laced with kindness.

Releasing the Anger

Father God, help me obey Your commands, for obedience leads to unmatched blessings. And one thing You ask of those who love You is to rein in their anger. Losing my temper ushers in dissension and destruction. You also want me to steer clear of vengeful thoughts and plots because they often flow from annoyance. In Your economy, there's no place for envy or jealousy, for they whisper lies into my heart that are hard to untangle and resentment usually follows. Instead, we're to live a holy and righteous life, trusting You to be the judge and jury on our behalf.

With Your help, today will be a better day. My heart is softened and ready to release the offenses I've held on to like a badge of honor. I don't want to be the angry woman always ready to grind the ax. Transform my fury into faith. In Jesus' name. Amen.

Stay away from anger and revenge. Keep envy far from you, for it only leads you into lies. For one day the wicked will be destroyed, but those who trust in the Lord will inherit the land.

PSALM 37:8–9 TPT

TODAY'S FOCUS POINT

Release anger into God's hands.

Learning Joy

Father God, I need to be around people who are full of happiness and joy. Not only is it contagious, but it also challenges me to see the good in the hard. Life doesn't have to be perfect to be amazing, and sometimes I need friends to remind me of that. I want to surround myself with women who have happy hearts because it's good medicine.

Today, bring people into my life who radiate joy. I want to learn how to let joy rule rather than sit in my sometimes-broken spirit and mope. I want to understand how to hold on to joy even when life is difficult and scary. I want my default button to any circumstance to be a happy heart and a cheerful mind because I know You're with me. So open my heart to learn how to rise above the heartache and cling to happiness and hope instead. God, You make the valleys and mountaintops of life not only tolerable but also teachable. In Jesus' name. Amen.

A happy heart is good medicine and a cheerful mind
works healing, but a broken spirit dries up the bones.
PROVERBS 17:22 AMPC

TODAY'S FOCUS POINT

Ask God for a happy heart.

Being Content No Matter What

Father God, I'm tired of being tossed around on waves that flow in and out of my life. I can't seem to find my footing, and it's frustrating. One moment I'm feeling safe and secure, and in the next, something happens and I'm completely destabilized. I feel satisfied with everything one day and then wake up anxious. Please help me find a place of comfort.

I want to be like Paul, who was able to find contentment no matter his circumstances. What a beautiful and mature faith to strive for. So help me learn to enjoy when life is full as well as when life is empty. Teach me ways to find Your goodness when I feel crushed and when I feel free. With You, there's simply no reason to be tossed around. Let me anchor my rest and contentment to You. In Jesus' name. Amen.

I am not saying this because I am in need. I have learned to be content in whatever circumstances. I know how to survive in tight situations, and I know how to enjoy having plenty. In fact, I have learned how to face any circumstances: fed or hungry, with or without.
PHILIPPIANS 4:11–12 VOICE

TODAY'S FOCUS POINT

Contentment is key to peace.

The Promise of Protection

Father God, show me Your kindness today. In the middle of my messy emotions, be faithful to save and restore. Protect me from every evil trying to distract me from living a faithful and fruitful life. It seems at every turn lately, there's another trap set to take me out. There are situations trying to stir up fear in me. And it seems certain people are laser focused on stirring me up. In my own strength, I'm failing.

Yet You are a trustworthy God who promises to strengthen me when I feel weak. You're always ready to pull me from the muck and mire, setting my feet on a firm foundation. And in Your Word, it's clear You promise to protect us from enemy schemes. You pledge to guard me from harm. So today, I'm asking You to make good on these promises by defending my heart and showing me how to navigate the choppy waters of my circumstances. I know You will. In Jesus' name. Amen.

But the Lord is faithful, and He will strengthen you [setting you on a firm foundation] and will protect and guard you from the evil one.
2 THESSALONIANS 3:3 AMP

TODAY'S FOCUS POINT

God is my protector and guardian.

Pleasing God

Father God, help me keep my eye on the prize of eternal life. Help me focus on You so intently that I don't look left or right, but instead follow in Your footsteps as they lead me to walk out my calling. And in whatever I do or say, let my life be a spotlight on Your goodness. My greatest desire is to please You. My hope is always to feel Your approval.

So as I speak to others today, keep my lips from saying words that distract attention from Your message of truth. Let me be pure in motive so I don't dilute the words You've given me to share. I want only Your name magnified through my life choices. And when I make mistakes, I want Your love and approval to set me back on track with a powerful testimony of Your goodness. My goal isn't to please others. My goal is to encourage them with the life-giving words they need to live in freedom and victory. In Jesus' name. Amen.

I'm obviously not trying to flatter you or water down my message to be popular with men, but my supreme passion is to please God. For if all I attempt to do is please people, I would fail to be a true servant of Christ.
GALATIANS 1:10 TPT

TODAY'S FOCUS POINT

Are my actions pleasing God?

A Calm, Cool Spirit

Father God, in Your Word You talk so often about the importance of being a peacemaker. You even go as far as to call peacemakers *blessed*. And while there are times to have righteous anger, to advocate, and to draw immovable lines in the sand, Your hope for me is to bring calmness whenever possible. As I have seen a million times, flaring tempers only make things worse. They rob me of civil discussions. And they break down the ability to effectively communicate and often ruin important relationships.

Today, would You give me the ability to navigate life with a calm, cool spirit? Bless me to be composed and unruffled. I'm not asking to sit it out. I don't want a life of avoidance. I don't want to be apathetic. But too often, I've been the one to create a caustic environment when there didn't need to be. Forgive me! Let me be a peacemaker moving forward. Let my presence bring a calmness because Your presence radiates from within me. In Jesus' name. Amen.

Hot tempers start fights; a calm, cool spirit keeps the peace.
PROVERBS 15:18 MSG

TODAY'S FOCUS POINT

Be a peacemaker whenever possible.

When I Struggle in the Waiting

Father God, when I get impatient as I wait for You, my heart is anything but quiet. I feel panicky, like I can't get a good, deep breath. I obsess over details I can't sway in my direction. I project negative outcomes down the road. I become angry thinking evil may win out. And I find myself overcome with a nagging sense of hopelessness. Help me!

But when I take a breath and pray, focusing on Your beautiful presence in my life, I find immediate relief. It allows my faith to catch up to my fear. I want to be more patient. . .more trusting. I want to believe in You always, knowing You're working behind the scenes for my benefit and Your glory. As it should be! So today, help my unbelief because I am too eager. Settle my anxious heart because I'm edgy and irritated. And quiet my heart as I take my worry to You. In Jesus' name. Amen.

Quiet your heart in his presence and wait patiently for Yahweh. And don't think for a moment that the wicked, in their prosperity, are better off than you.
PSALM 37:7 TPT

TODAY'S FOCUS POINT

Trust that God is working in the waiting.

Subject Index